Leisure and Positive Psychology

DOI: 10.1057/9781137569943.0001

Other Palgrave Pivot titles

Simon Massey and Rino Coluccello: **Eurafrican Migration: Legal, Economic and Social Responses to Irregular Migration**

Duncan McDuie-Ra: **Debating Race in Contemporary India**

Andrea Greenbaum: **The Tropes of War: Visual Hyperbole and Spectacular Culture**

Kristoffer Kropp: **A Historical Account of Danish Sociology: A Troubled Sociology**

Monika E. Reuter: **Creativity – A Sociological Approach**

M. Saiful Islam: **Pursuing Alternative Development: Indigenous People, Ethnic Organization and Agency**

Justin DePlato: **American Presidential Power and the War on Terror: Does the Constitution Matter?**

Christopher Perkins: **The United Red Army on Screen: Cinema, Aesthetics and The Politics of Memory**

Susanne Lundin: **Organs for Sale: An Ethnographic Examination of the International Organ Trade**

Margot Finn and Kate Smith: **New Paths to Public Histories**

Vicky Duckworth and Gordon Ade-Ojo: **Adult Literacy Policy and Practice: From Intrinsic Values to Instrumentalism**

Brendan Howe: **Democratic Governance in Northeast Asia: A Human-Centred Approach to Evaluating Democracy**

Evie Kendal: **Equal Opportunity and the Case for State Sponsored Ectogenesis**

Joseph Watras: **Philosophies of Environmental Education and Democracy: Harris, Dewey, and Bateson on Human Freedoms in Nature**

Christos Kourtelis: **The Political Economy of Euro-Mediterranean Relations: European Neighbourhood Policy in North Africa**

Liz Montegary and Melissa Autumn White (editors): **Mobile Desires: The Politics and Erotics of Mobility Justice**

Anna Larsson and Sanja Magdalenić: **Sociology in Sweden: A History**

Philip Whitehead: **Reconceptualising the Moral Economy of Criminal Justice: A New Perspective**

Robert Kerr: **How Postmodernism Explains Football and Football Explains Postmodernism: The Billy Clyde Conundrum**

Ilan Bijaoui: **The Open Incubator Model: Entrepreneurship, Open Innovation, and Economic Development in the Periphery**

DOI: 10.1057/9781137569943.0001

palgrave▸pivot

Leisure and Positive Psychology: Linking Activities with Positiveness

Robert A. Stebbins
Professor Emeritus, University of Calgary, Canada

palgrave
macmillan

DOI: 10.1057/9781137569943.0001

First published 2015 by
PALGRAVE MACMILLAN

Palgrave Macmillan in the UK is an imprint of Macmillan Publishers Limited, registered in England, company number 785998, of Houndmills, Basingstoke, Hampshire RG21 6XS.

Palgrave Macmillan in the US is a division of St Martin's Press LLC, 175 Fifth Avenue, New York, NY 10010.

Palgrave Macmillan is the global academic imprint of the above companies and has companies and representatives throughout the world.

Palgrave® and Macmillan® are registered trademarks in the United States, the United Kingdom, Europe and other countries.

ISBN: 978–1–137–56995–0 EPUB
ISBN: 978–1–137–56994–3 PDF
ISBN: 978–1–137–56993–6 Hardback

A catalogue record for this book is available from the British Library.

A catalog record for this book is available from the Library of Congress.

www.palgrave.com/pivot

DOI: 10.1057/9781137569943

Contents

Acknowledgments

My sincere thanks go to Vidhya Jayaprakash and the production team at Newgen Knowledge Works and to Palgrave Macmillan's editors Harriet Barker and Amelia Derkatsch for efficiently shepherding it through the various stages of acquisition and production.

DOI: 10.1057/9781137569943.0002

Introduction

Abstract: *Leisure plays a key role in positive psychology, though it would be difficult to reach this conclusion from the infrequency with which the idea surfaces in the field's publications and intellectual discussions. This book shows how theory and research from the interdisciplinary field of leisure studies, more specifically from the serious leisure perspective (SLP), can be used to join the two fields, which have so much to offer each other. Thus, positive interpersonal relationships and positive emotional and cognitive states and processes – the stuff of positive psychology – are expressed or realized in myriad leisure activities (i.e., sets of particular behaviors). These activities are highly appealing, thereby providing their own motivational push. Leisure is defined and conceptualized as a kind of activity. General activities include the pursuit of certain core activities, which constitute powerful reasons for engaging in such leisure.*

Keywords: activity; agency; leisure; positive psychology; role; serious leisure perspective

Stebbins, Robert A. *Leisure and Positive Psychology: Linking Activities with Positiveness.* Basingstoke: Palgrave Macmillan, 2015. DOI: 10.1057/9781137569943.0003.

Leisure has a central role to play in positive psychology, though it would be difficult to reach this conclusion from the infrequency with which the idea surfaces in the latter field's publications and intellectual discussions. This is odd, for many of positive psychology's most vibrant ideas are equally prominent in the domain of leisure and its analytic home, leisure studies. These ideas include flow, fulfillment, altruism, well-being, and interpersonal relationships. Moreover, there should be much greater discourse between the two fields, since leisure studies has a variety of well-validated conceptual tools that can help positive psychology find its proper and rightful place in the domain of free time. Indeed, until positive psychology came along, leisure studies could justifiably claim to be the only positive social science.

This may sound audacious, coming as it is from a sociologist, albeit one whose minor in graduate studies was psychology (I also took as an undergraduate a double major in sociology and psychology). More to the point, however, is that my intellectual base for the past 40 years has been in leisure studies. It is a broad interdiscipline composed primarily of psychology and sociology as well as geography, education, economics, history, and philosophy. As I intend to explain in the following pages, leisure is a vast domain, and with two other more or less equally vast domains – work and nonwork obligation – covers every aspect of human existence. This domainal framework is set out elsewhere (Stebbins, 2009, chap. 1), where I also present a positive sociology as inspired by the advances in the study of positiveness made in positive psychology.

What has become clear to me over the past 40 years is that leisure is an important feature of many areas of life, some of which might appear at first blush to be unrelated. By way of example, consider therapeutic recreation, where leisure is used to help people with disabilities find an agreeable lifestyle. Consider arts and science administration, where volunteers make significant contributions as instructors and members of boards of directors. Consider library and information science, where leisure theory is helping specialists understand how information is gathered and disseminated in that domain of free time. Consider tourism studies and event analysis, where participants, all in search of some kind of leisure, have a range of different motives for spending their free time here. In brief, the study of leisure has since around 1970 resulted in a solid and widely applicable body of knowledge.

This book shows how theory and research from the interdiscipline of leisure studies, more specifically from the serious leisure perspective

DOI: 10.1057/9781137569943.0003

(SLP), can be used to join the two fields, which have so much to offer each other. In this regard the present book may be seen as a next step following on Teresa Freire's *Positive Leisure Science* (2013). Her anthology shows generally the critical role of leisure in the study and application of positiveness. In the present volume I want to link, in more particular fashion, the SLP, its central concept of activity, and positive psychology. Bear in mind that this is in no way an attempt to merge the two fields theoretically and empirically into one overarching conceptual framework. This would be an immense undertaking and, at this stage of their development, very probably an impossible one.

Why use the SLP to meet this goal? One reason, perhaps selfish, is that I have been its prime mover since its inception in 1973 (a short history is available at www.seriousleisure.net). We academics find much positiveness in promoting our own ideas. More important for this book, however, is that this perspective is the only theoretic framework in leisure studies that bears in some way on most, if not all, of that field. It offers the widest lens for viewing leisure, even while a number of other theories offer more detailed looks at certain aspects of it (e.g., leisure constraints, recreational specialization, and social-class analysis).

I will argue that positive interpersonal relationships and positive emotional and cognitive states and processes – the stuff of positive psychology – are expressed or realized in myriad leisure activities (i.e., sets of particular behaviors). These activities are highly appealing, thereby providing their own motivational push. The more complicated of them (the serious pursuits) are, in turn, rooted in surrounding social worlds of people, groups, organizations, services, and a unique history. A powerful personal and social identity typically follows from involvement in these activities.

What is leisure?

Leisure is uncoerced, contextually framed activity engaged in during free time, which people want to do and, using their abilities and resources, actually do in either a satisfying or a fulfilling way, if not both (the definition of leisure is considered at length in Stebbins, 2012, p. 4). "Free time" in this definition is time away from unpleasant, or disagreeable, obligation, with pleasant obligation being treated of here as essentially leisure. In other words *homo otiosus* (Stebbins, 2013), leisure man, feels

DOI: 10.1057/9781137569943.0003

no significant coercion to enact the activity in question. Some kinds of work, referred to here as "devotee work," can be conceived of as pleasant obligation, in that such workers though they must make a living at their work, do so in a highly intrinsically appealing pursuit. Work of this sort is also essentially leisure, and will be regarded as such in this book. This definition is compatible with the SLP, particularly since the latter stresses human agency, or "intentionality" (Rojek, 2010, p. 6), – what "people want to do" – and distinguishes the satisfaction gained from casual leisure vis-à-vis the fulfillment flowing from the serious form.

Note that reference to "free choice" – a long-standing component of standard definitions of leisure – is, for reasons, discussed more fully elsewhere (Stebbins, 2005 intentionally omitted from this definition. Generally put, choice is never wholly free, but rather hedged about with all sorts of conditions. This situation renders this concept and allied ones such as freedom and state of mind useless as essential elements of a basic definition (Juniu & Henderson, 2001). Note, too, that there is no reference in this definition to the moral basis of leisure as one of its distinguishing features; in other words, contrary to some stances taken in the past (e.g., Kaplan, 1960, pp. 22–25), leisure according to the SLP may be either deviant or nondeviant (see next chapter).

Uncoerced, people in leisure believe that they are doing something they are not pushed to do, something they are not disagreeably obliged to do. In this definition emphasis is ipso facto on the acting individual and the play of human agency. This in no way denies that there may be things people want to do but cannot do because of any number of constraints on choice, because of limiting social and personal conditions; for example, aptitude, ability, socialized leisure tastes, knowledge of available activities, and accessibility of activities. In other words, when using this definition of leisure, whose central ingredient is lack of coercion, we must be sure to understand leisure activities in relation to their larger personal, structural, cultural, and historical background, their context. And it follows that leisure is not really freely chosen, as some observers have claimed (e.g., Parker, 1983, pp. 8–9; Kelly, 1990, p. 7), since choice of activity is significantly shaped by this background.

Nor may free time, as conventionally defined, be treated of here as synonymous with leisure. We can be bored in our free time, which can result from inactivity ("nothing to do") or from activity, which alas, is uninteresting, unstimulating. The same can, of course, happen at work and in obligated nonwork settings. Since boredom is a decidedly

DOI: 10.1057/9781137569943.0003

negative state of mind, it can be argued that, logically, it is not leisure at all. For leisure is typically conceived of as a positive mind set, composed of, among other sentiments, pleasant expectations and recollections of activities and situations. Of course, it happens at times that expectations turn out to be unrealistic, and we get bored (or perhaps angry, frightened, or embarrassed) with the activity in question, transforming it in our view into something quite other than leisure. And all this may happen in free time, which exemplifies well how such time can occupy a broader area of life than leisure, which is nested within it (Stebbins, 2003).

Leisure as activity

Our condensed definition refers to "un-coerced activity." An activity is a type of pursuit, wherein participants in it mentally or physically (often both) think or do something, motivated by the hope of achieving a desired end. Psychologically, an activity is a set of behaviors sufficiently coordinated to reach the end. Life is filled with activities, both pleasant and unpleasant: sleeping, mowing the lawn, taking the train to work, having a tooth filled, eating lunch, playing tennis matches, running a meeting, and on and on. Activities, as this list illustrates, may be categorized as work, leisure, or nonwork obligation. They are, furthermore, general. In some instances they refer to the behavioral side of recognizable roles, for example commuter, tennis player, and chair of a meeting. In others we may recognize the activity but not conceive of it so formally as a role, exemplified in someone sleeping, mowing a lawn, or eating lunch (not as patron in a restaurant).

The concept of activity is an abstraction, and as such, one broader than that of role. In other words roles are associated with particular statuses, or positions, in society, whereas with activities, some are status based while others are not. For instance, sleeper is not a status, even if sleeping is an activity. It is likewise with lawn mower (person). Sociologists, anthropologists, and psychologists tend to see social relations in terms of roles, and as a result, overlook activities whether aligned with a role or not. Meanwhile certain important parts of life consist of engaging in activities not recognized as roles. Where would many of us be could we not routinely sleep or eat lunch?

Moreover another dimension separates role and activity, namely, that of statics and dynamics. Roles are static whereas activities are

DOI: 10.1057/9781137569943.0003

dynamic.[1] Roles, classically conceived of, are relatively inactive expectations for behavior, whereas in activities, people are actually behaving, mentally or physically thinking or doing things to achieve certain ends. This dynamic quality provides a powerful explanatory link between an activity and a person's motivation to participate in it. Nevertheless the idea of role is useful in positive psychology, since participants do encounter role expectations in certain activities (e.g., those in sport, work, volunteering). Although the concept of activity does not include these expectations, in its dynamism, it can, much more effectively than role, account for invention and human agency.

This definition of activity gets further refined in the concept of core activity: a distinctive set of interrelated actions or steps that must be followed to achieve the outcome or product that the participant seeks. As with general activities core activities are pursued in work, leisure, and nonwork obligation. Consider some examples in serious leisure: a core activity of alpine skiing is descending snow-covered slopes, in cabinet making it is shaping and finishing wood, and in volunteer fire fighting is putting out blazes and rescuing people from them. In each case the participant takes several interrelated steps to successfully ski downhill, make a cabinet, or rescue someone. In casual leisure core activities, which are much less complex than in serious leisure, are exemplified in the actions required to hold sociable conversations with friends, savor beautiful scenery, and offer simple volunteer services (e.g., handing out leaflets, directing traffic in a theater parking lot, clearing snow off the neighborhood hockey rink). Work-related core activities are seen in, for instance, the actions of a surgeon during an operation or the improvisations on a melody by a jazz clarinetist. The core activity in mowing a lawn (nonwork obligation) is pushing or riding the mower. Executing an attractive core activity and its component steps and actions is a main feature drawing participants to the general activity encompassing it, because this core directly enables them to reach a cherished goal. It is the opposite for disagreeable core activities. In short the core activity has motivational value of its own, even if more strongly held for some activities than others and even if some activities are disagreeable but still have to be done.

Core activities can be classified as simple or complex, the two concepts finding their place at opposite poles of a continuum. The location of a core activity on this continuum partially explains its appeal or lack thereof. Most casual leisure is comprised of a set of simple core activities. Here *homo otiosus* need only turn on the television set, observe the scenery, drink the glass of wine (no oenophile is he), or gossip about someone. Complexity in casual leisure increases slightly when playing a board game using dice, participating in a Hash House Harrier treasure hunt, or serving as a casual volunteer by, say, collecting bottles for the Scouts or making tea and coffee after a religious service. And Harrison's (2001) study of upper-middle-class Canadian mass tourists revealed a certain level of complexity in their sensual experience of the touristic sites they visited. For people craving the simple things in life, this is the kind of leisure to head for. The other two domains abound with equivalent simple core activities, as in the work of a parking lot attendant (receiving cash/making change) or the efforts of a householder whose nonwork obligation of the day is raking leaves.

So, if complexity is what people want, they must look elsewhere. Leisure projects are necessarily more complex than casual leisure activities. The types of projects listed in Chapter 2 provide, I believe, ample proof of that. Nonetheless, they are not nearly as complex as the core activities around which serious leisure revolves. The accumulated knowledge, skill, training, and experience of, for instance, the amateur trumpet player, hobbyist stamp collector, and volunteer emergency medical worker are vast, and defy full description of how they are applied during conduct of the core activity. Of course, neophytes in the serious leisure activities lack these acquisitions, though it is unquestionably their intention to acquire them to a level where they will feel fulfilled. As with simple core activities complex equivalents also exist in the other two domains. Examples in work include the two earlier examples of the surgeon and jazz clarinetist. In the nonwork domain two common examples demonstrate a noticeable level of complexity: driving in city traffic and (for many people) preparing the annual income tax return.

Can all of life be characterized as an endless unfolding of activities? Probably not. For instance, the definition of activity does not fit things some people are, through violence, compelled to experience entirely against their will, including rape, torture, interrogation, forced feeding, and judicial execution. It would seem to be likewise for the actions of those driven by a compulsive mental disorder. There are also comparatively more benign situations in which most people still feel compelled to participate, among them, enduring receipt of a roadside traffic citation or a bawling out from the boss. Both fail to qualify as activities. In all these examples the ends sought are those of other people, as they pursue their

DOI: 10.1057/9781137569943.0003

activities. Meanwhile the "victims" lack agency, unless they can manage to counterattack with an activity of resistance.

Activity as just defined is, by and large, a foreign idea in psychology, anthropology, and sociology. Sure, scholars there sometimes talk about, for instance, criminal, political, or economic activity, but in so doing, they are referring, in general terms, to a broad category of behavior, not a particular set of actions comprising a pursuit. Instead the foregoing positive conception of activity knows its greatest currency in the interdisciplinary fields of leisure studies and physical education and, more recently, kinesiology. And I suspect that the first adopted the idea from the second. There has always been, in physical education, discussion of and research on activities promoting conditioning, exercise, outdoor interests, human movement, and the like.

Leisure as positive activity

Positiveness is a personal sentiment felt by people who pursue those things in life they desire, the things they do to make their existence, rewarding, attractive, and therefore worth living (Seligman & Csikszentmihalyi, 2000; Stebbins, 2009). Such people feel positive about these aspects of life. Because of this sentiment they may also feel positive toward life in general. A primary focus of positive social scientific research is on how, when, where, and why people pursue those things in life that they desire, on the things they do to create a worthwhile existence that, in combination, is substantially rewarding, satisfying, and fulfilling. General and core activities, sometimes joined with role, most of the time agreeable, but sometimes momentarily disagreeable, form the cornerstone of leisure. It is through certain activities that people, propelled by their own agency, find positive things in life, which they blend and balance with certain negative things they must also deal with. All this is carried out in the three previously mentioned domains of work, nonwork obligation, and leisure.

In other words this book shows, using leisure as its point of departure, that love, fulfillment, creativity, and so on, are more than personal emotions or feelings. They are simultaneously social phenomena rooted in the domain of leisure that encompasses them, knowledge of which further explains these emotions and sentiments. The large question asked in this book is where do positive sentiments, attitudes, processes, and the

DOI: 10.1057/9781137569943.0003

like take place. It also addresses itself to two subsidiary questions of how and when do positive activities occur. This agenda complements positive psychology, which has tended to concentrate on who experiences these sentiments, attitudes, and so on, and why this happens.

Chapter 1 contains a basic statement of the SLP, with special emphasis throughout on positiveness. I introduce Chapters 2 through 9 with a discussion of some of the relevant emotions that follow from the positive phenomena considered there. Next the phenomena themselves are set out in some detail and linked to the SLP, always guided by the intention of showing with some precision how positiveness fits with free time. These phenomena are the following: Chapter 2, the serious pursuits; Chapter 3, interpersonal relationships; Chapter 4, contemplation and spirituality; Chapter 5, altruism; Chapter 6, contribution to community; Chapter 7, well-being (happiness); Chapter 8, casual and project-based leisure; and Chapter 9, play and creativity.

This book is, at bottom, a conceptual undertaking; my goal being to show how the various leisure activities fit in positive psychology along the lines of many of its central concepts. It is not my intention to try to confirm these conceptual links by drawing on existing data, since data *effectively* linking positive phenomena with particular leisure activities are rare. That is, in such research either the positive psychological states or the leisure activities tend to be weakly conceptualized. Rather, this book serves as a call to action, as a rallying cry for studies that looks directly at positive states and processes as sought and experienced in particular free-time pursuits. In such research the states, processes, and pursuits must be carefully conceptualized with reference to each other.

Note

1 I am aware that general sociological and psychological theory conceives of roles as dynamic and statuses as static. Compared with activities, however, roles are relatively static.

References

Freire, T. (Ed.) (2013). *Positive leisure science: From subjective experience to social contexts.* Dordrecht, the Netherlands: Springer.

DOI: 10.1057/9781137569943.0003

Harrison, J. (2001). Thinking about tourists. *International Sociology*, 16, 159–172.
Juniu, S., & Henderson, K. (2001). Problems in researching leisure and women: Global considerations. *World Leisure Journal*, 43(4), 3–10.
Kaplan, M. (1960). *Leisure in America: A social inquiry*. New York: John Wiley.
Kelly, J.R. (1990). *Leisure*, 2nd ed. Englewood Cliffs, NJ: Prentice-Hall.
Parker, S. (1983). *Leisure and work*. London: George Allen & Unwin.
Rojek, C. (2010). *The labour of leisure*. London: Sage.
Seligman, M.E.P., & Csikszentmihalyi, M. (2000). Positive psychology: An introduction. *American Psychologist*, 55(1), 5–14.
Stebbins, R.A. (2003). Boredom in free time. *Leisure Studies Association Newsletter*, 64(March), 29–31. (also available at www.seriousleisure.net – Digital Library, "Leisure Reflections No. 2").
Stebbins, R.A. (2005). Choice and experiential definitions of leisure. *Leisure Sciences*, 27, 349–352.
Stebbins, R.A. (2009). *Personal decisions in the public square: Beyond problem solving into a positive sociology*. New Brunswick, NJ: Transaction.
Stebbins, R.A. (2012). *The idea of leisure: First principles*. New Brunswick, NJ: Transaction.
Stebbins, R.A. (2013). *Homo otiosus*: Who is this creature, does it exist, should it matter? *Leisure Studies Association Newsletter*, 94(March): 19–21 at (also available at www.seriousleisure.net/Digital Library, "Leisure Reflections No. 32").

DOI: 10.1057/9781137569943.0003

1
The Serious Leisure Perspective

Abstract: *The serious leisure perspective (SLP) can be described, in simplest terms, as the theoretical framework that synthesizes three main forms of leisure showing, at once, their distinctive features, similarities, and interrelationships. The forms consist of the (1) serious pursuits (i.e., serious leisure [amateurism, hobbyism, and serious volunteering] and devotee work), (2) casual leisure, and (3) project-based leisure. The serious pursuits are distinguished by six qualities, are motivated by several special rewards, sometimes including flow, and offer a leisure career. Eight types of casual leisure are presented along with their benefits. Project-based leisure fits into leisure lifestyle in its own peculiar way as interstitial activity, like some casual leisure but not like most serious leisure. It can therefore help shape a person's optimal leisure lifestyle.*

Keywords: Amateurs; casual leisure; devotee work; flow; hobbyists; leisure career; project-based leisure; serious leisure; serious leisure perspective; volunteers

Stebbins, Robert A. *Leisure and Positive Psychology: Linking Activities with Positiveness.* Basingstoke: Palgrave Macmillan, 2015. DOI: 10.1057/9781137569943.0004.

The serious leisure perspective (SLP) can be described, in simplest terms, as the theoretical framework that synthesizes three main forms of leisure showing, at once, their distinctive features, similarities, and interrelationships (the SLP is discussed in detail in Stebbins, 2007/2015; 2001a; 1992). Additionally the Perspective (wherever Perspective appears as shorthand for SLP, to avoid confusion, the first letter will be capitalized) considers how the three forms – serious pursuits (serious leisure/devotee work), casual leisure, and project-based leisure – are shaped by various psychological, social, cultural, and historical conditions. Each form serves as a conceptual umbrella for a range of types of related activities. That the Perspective takes its name from the first of these should, in no way, suggest that it be regarded, in some abstract sense, as the most important or superior of the three. Rather the Perspective is so titled, simply because it got its start in the study of serious leisure; such leisure is, strictly from the standpoint of intellectual invention, the godfather of the other two. Furthermore serious leisure has become the benchmark from which analyses of casual and project-based leisure have often been undertaken. So naming the Perspective after the first facilitates intellectual recognition; it keeps the idea in familiar territory for all concerned.

My research findings and theoretical musings over the past 40 years have nevertheless evolved and coalesced into a typological map of the world of leisure (for a brief history of the Perspective, see the history page at www.seriousleisure.net or for a longer version, see Stebbins, 2007/2015, chap. 6). That is, so far as known at present, all leisure (at least in Western society) can be classified according to one of the three forms and their several types and subtypes. More precisely the SLP offers a classification and explanation of all leisure activities and experiences, as these two are framed in the psychological, social, cultural, geographical, and historical conditions in which each activity and accompanying experience take place.

DOI: 10.1057/9781137569943.0004

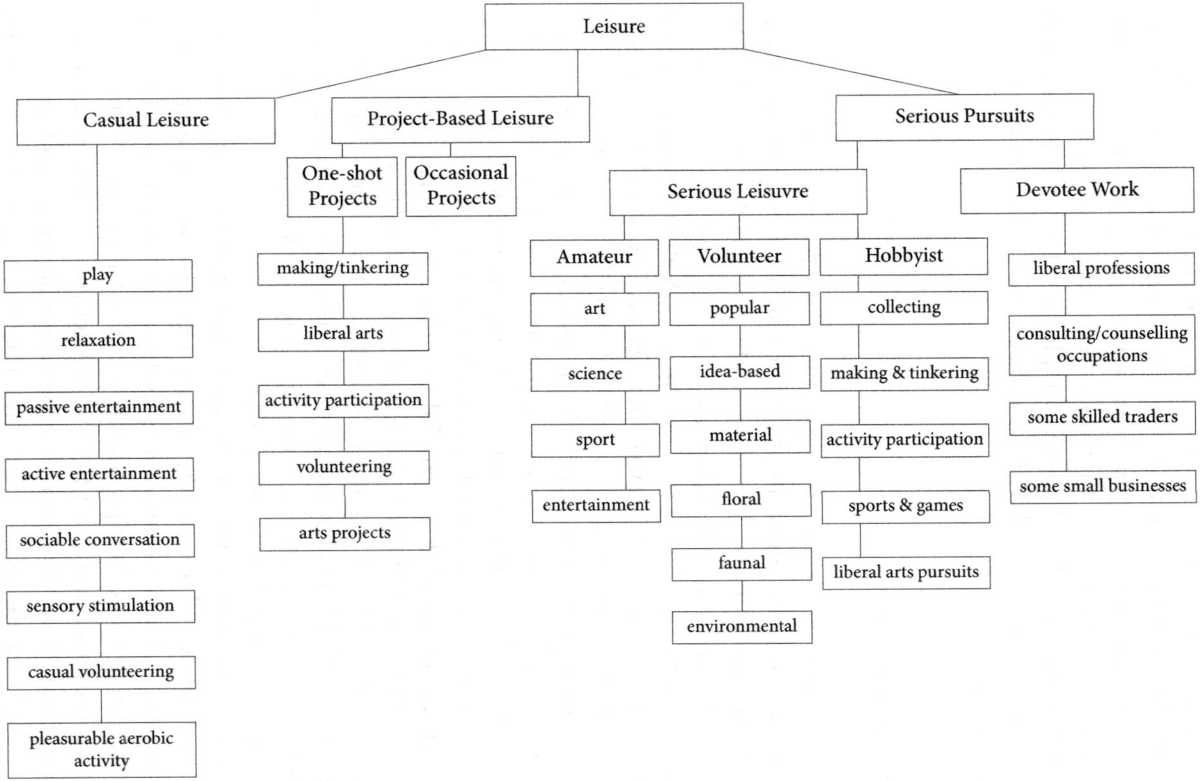

FIGURE 1.1 *The serious leisure perspective*

source: Diagram formulated by Jenna Hartel

Serious pursuits

In this chapter serious leisure and devotee work are placed under the heading of serious pursuits, as its two types. The present chapter explains this classificatory change, from what was to this point in the history of the SLP a separation of the two as leisure and work, respectively. The justification for this change is simple: devotee work is essentially leisure. So we should call this spade a spade and explore it as part of the Perspective.

Serious leisure

Serious leisure, one of the two types of serious pursuit, is the systematic pursuit of an amateur, hobbyist, or volunteer activity sufficiently substantial, interesting, and fulfilling for the participant to find a (leisure) career there acquiring and expressing a combination of its special skills, knowledge, and experience. I coined the term (Stebbins, 1982) to express the way the people he interviewed and observed viewed the importance of these three kinds of activity in their everyday lives. The adjective "serious" (a word my research respondents often used) embodies such qualities as earnestness, sincerity, importance, and carefulness, rather than gravity, solemnity, joylessness, distress, and anxiety. Although the second set of terms occasionally describes serious leisure events, they are uncharacteristic of them and fail to nullify, or, in many cases, even dilute, the overall fulfillment gained by the participants. The idea of "career" in this definition follows sociological tradition, where careers are seen as available in all substantial, complex roles, including those in leisure. Finally, as we shall see shortly, serious leisure is distinct from casual leisure and project-based leisure.

Amateurs are found in art, science, sport, and entertainment, where they are invariably linked in a variety of ways with professional counterparts. The two can be distinguished descriptively in that the activity in question constitutes a livelihood for professionals but not amateurs. Furthermore, most professionals work full-time at the activity whereas all amateurs pursue it part-time. The part-time professionals in art and entertainment complicate this picture; although they work part-time, their work is judged by other professionals and by the amateurs as of professional quality. Amateurs and professionals are locked in and therefore defined

DOI: 10.1057/9781137569943.0004

by a system of relations linking them and their publics – the "professional-amateur-public system," or P-A-P system (discussed in more detail in Stebbins, 2007/2015, pp. 6–8, including Yoder's [1997] addition of the C-PC-AP system). But note here that enactment of the core activity by the professionals in a particular field, to influence amateurs there, must be sufficiently visible to those amateurs. If the amateurs, in general, have no idea of the prowess of their professional counterparts, the latter become irrelevant as role models, and the leisure side of the activity remains at a hobbyist level.

Hobbyists lack this professional alter ego, suggesting that, historically, all amateurs were hobbyists before their fields professionalized. Both types are drawn to their leisure pursuits significantly more by self-interest than by altruism, whereas volunteers engage in activities requiring a more or less equal blend of these two motives. Hobbyists may be classified in five types: collectors, makers and tinkerers, noncompetitive activity participants (e.g., fishing, hiking, orienteering), hobbyist sports and games (e.g., ultimate Frisbee, croquet, gin rummy), and the liberal arts hobbies.

The liberal arts hobbyists are enamored of the systematic acquisition of knowledge for its own sake. Many of them accomplish this by reading voraciously in a field of art, sport, cuisine, language, culture, history, science, philosophy, politics, or literature (Stebbins, 1994). But some of them go beyond this to expand their knowledge still further through cultural tourism, documentary videos, television programs, and similar resources. Although the matter has yet to be studied through research, it is theoretically possible to separate buffs from consumers in the liberal arts hobbies of sport, cuisine, and the fine and entertainment arts. Some people – call them *consumers* – more or less uncritically consume restaurant fare, sports events, or displays of art (concerts, shows, exhibitions) as pure entertainment and sensory stimulation (casual leisure), whereas others – call them *buffs* – participate in these same situations as more or less knowledgeable experts, as serious leisure (for more on this distinction, see Stebbins, 2002, chap. 5). The ever rarer Renaissance man of our day may also be classified here, even though such people avoid specializing in one field of learning to acquire, instead, a somewhat more superficial knowledge of a variety of fields. Being broadly well-read is a (liberal arts) hobby of its own.

What have been referred to as "the nature-challenge activities" (Davidson & Stebbins, 2011) fall primarily under the hobbyist heading of noncompetitive, rule-based activity participation. True, actual competitions are sometimes held in, for instance, snowboarding, kayaking, and mountain biking (e.g., fastest time over a particular course), but mostly beating nature is thrill enough. Moreover, other nature hobbies exist, which are also challenging, but in very different ways. Some, most notably fishing and hunting, in essence exploit the natural environment. Still others center on appreciation of the outdoors, among them hiking, backpacking, bird watching, and horseback riding.

Volunteering is uncoerced, intentionally productive, altruistic activity engaged in during free time. Engaged in as leisure, it is, thus, activity that people want to do (Stebbins, 2013). It is through volunteer work – it is done in either an informal or a formal setting – that these people provide a service or benefit to one or more individuals (who must be outside that person's family). Usually volunteers receive no pay, though people serving in volunteer programs are sometimes compensated for out-of-pocket expenses. Moreover, in the field of nonprofit studies, since no volunteer work is involved, giving, say, blood, money, or clothing as an altruistic act is not, strictly speaking, volunteering. Meanwhile, in the typical case, volunteers who are altruistically providing a service or benefit to others are themselves also benefiting from various rewards experienced during this process (e.g., pleasant social interaction, self-enriching experiences, sense of contributing to nonprofit group success). In other words volunteering is motivated by two basic attitudes: altruism *and* self-interest.

The conception of volunteering that squares best with our interest in leisure and positiveness revolves, in significant part, around a central subjective motivational question: it must be determined whether volunteers feel they are engaging in an enjoyable (casual leisure), fulfilling (serious leisure), or enjoyable or fulfilling (project-based leisure) core activity that they have had the option to accept or reject on their own terms. A key element in the leisure conception of volunteering is the felt absence of coercion, moral or otherwise, to participate in the volunteer activity (Stebbins, 1996), an element that, in "marginal volunteering" (Stebbins, 2001), may be experienced in degrees, as more or less coercive. The reigning conception of volunteering in nonprofit sector research is not that of volunteering as leisure, but rather volunteering as unpaid work. The first – an *economic* conception – defines volunteering as the absence of payment as livelihood, whether in money or in kind. This definition, for the most part, leaves unanswered the messy question

DOI: 10.1057/9781137569943.0004

of motivation so crucial to the second, positive sociological, definition, which is a *volitional* conception.

Six qualities

The serious pursuits are further defined by six distinctive qualities, qualities uniformly found among its amateurs, hobbyists, and volunteers. One is the occasional need to *persevere*. Participants who want to continue experiencing the same level of fulfillment in the activity have to meet certain challenges from time to time. Thus, musicians must practice assiduously to master difficult musical passages, baseball players must throw repeatedly to perfect favorite pitches, and volunteers must search their imaginations for new approaches with which to help children with reading problems. It happens in all three types of serious leisure and in devotee work that deepest fulfillment sometimes comes at the end of the activity rather than during it, from sticking with it through thick and thin, from conquering adversity.

Another quality distinguishing all the serious pursuits is the opportunity to follow a (leisure, or leisure-work) *career* in the endeavor, a career shaped by its own special contingencies, turning points, and stages of achievement and involvement. A career that, in some fields, notably certain arts and sports, may nevertheless include decline. Moreover, most, if not all, careers here owe their existence to a third quality: serious leisure participants make significant personal *effort* using their specially acquired knowledge, training, or skill and, indeed at times, all three. Careers for serious leisure participants unfold along lines of their efforts to achieve, for instance, a high level of showmanship, athletic prowess, or scientific knowledge or to accumulate formative experiences in a volunteer role.

The serious pursuits are further distinguished by several durable benefits, or tangible, salutary outcomes such activity for its participants. They include self-actualization, self-enrichment, self-expression, self-fulfillment, regeneration or renewal of self, feelings of accomplishment, enhancement of self-image, social interaction and sense of belonging, and lasting physical products of the activity (e.g., a painting, scientific paper, piece of furniture). A further benefit – self-gratification, or pure fun, which is by far the most evanescent benefit in this list – is also enjoyed by casual leisure participants. The possibility of realizing such benefits constitutes a powerful goal in the serious pursuits.

DOI: 10.1057/9781137569943.0004

Fifth, each serious pursuit is distinguished by a unique *ethos* that emerges in parallel with each expression of it. An ethos is the spirit of the community of serious leisure/devotee work participants, as manifested in shared attitudes, practices, values, beliefs, goals, and so on. The social world of the participants is the organizational milieu in which the associated ethos – at bottom a cultural formation – is expressed (as attitudes, beliefs, values) or realized (as practices, goals). According to David Unruh (1979; 1980) every social world has its characteristic groups, events, routines, practices, and organizations. It is held together, to an important degree, by semiformal, or mediated, communication. In other words, in the typical case, social worlds are neither heavily bureaucratized nor substantially organized through intense face-to-face interaction. Rather, communication is commonly mediated by newsletters, posted notices, telephone messages, mass mailings, radio and television announcements, and similar means.

> Unruh (1980, p. 277) says of the social world that it must be seen as a unit of social organization which is diffuse and amorphous in character. Generally larger than groups or organizations, social worlds are not necessarily defined by formal boundaries, membership lists, or spatial territory.... A social world must be seen as an internally recognizable constellation of actors, organizations, events, and practices which have coalesced into a perceived sphere of interest and involvement for participants. Characteristically, a social world lacks a powerful centralized authority structure and is delimited by... effective communication and not territory nor formal group membership.

The social world is a diffuse, amorphous entity to be sure, but nevertheless one of great importance in the impersonal, segmented life of the modern urban community. Its importance is further amplified by a parallel element of the special ethos, which is missing from Unruh's conception, namely that such worlds are also constituted of a rich subculture. One function of this subculture is to interrelate the many components of this diffuse and amorphous entity. In other words, there is associated with each social world a set of special norms, values, beliefs, styles, moral principles, performance standards, and similar shared representations.

Every social world contains four types of members: strangers, tourists, regulars, and insiders (Unruh, 1979; 1980). The strangers are intermediaries who normally participate little in the leisure/work activity itself, but who nonetheless do something important to make it possible, for example, by managing municipal parks (in amateur baseball), minting coins (in hobbyist coin collecting), and organizing the work of teachers'

DOI: 10.1057/9781137569943.0004

aids (in career volunteering). Tourists are temporary participants in a social world; they have come on the scene momentarily for entertainment, diversion, or profit. Most amateur and hobbyist activities have publics of some kind, which are, at bottom, constituted of tourists. The clients of many volunteers can be similarly classified. The regulars routinely participate in the social world; in serious leisure, they are the amateurs, hobbyists, and volunteers themselves. The insiders are those among them who show exceptional devotion to the social world they share, to maintaining it, to advancing it. In the SLP such people are analyzed according to an involvement scale as either "core devotees" or "moderate devotees" and contrasted with "participants," or regulars (Stebbins, 2007/2015, pp. 20–21; Siegenthaler & O'Dell, 2003).

The sixth quality – participants in serious leisure tend to identify strongly with their chosen pursuits – springs from the presence of the other five distinctive qualities. In contrast, most casual leisure, although not usually humiliating or despicable, is nonetheless too fleeting, mundane, and commonplace to become the basis for a distinctive *identity* for most people.

Rewards, costs, and motivation

Furthermore certain rewards and costs come with pursuing a hobbyist, amateur, volunteer, or devotee work activity. Both implicitly and explicitly much of the SLP rests on the following assumption: to understand the meaning of this kind of work and leisure for those who pursue it is in good part to understand their motivation for the pursuit. Moreover, one fruitful approach to understanding the motives that lead to such involvement is to study them through the eyes of the participants who, past studies reveal (e.g., Stebbins, 1992, chap. 6; Arai & Pedlar, 1997), see it as a mix of offsetting costs and rewards experienced in the central activity. The rewards of this activity tend to outweigh the costs, however, the result being that the participants usually find a high level of personal fulfillment in them.

In these studies the participant's fulfillment (the equivalent of eudaemonia as used in modern psychology) has been found to stem from a constellation of particular rewards gained from the activity, be it boxing, ice climbing, or giving dance lessons to the elderly. Furthermore, the rewards are not only fulfilling in themselves, but also fulfilling as

DOI: 10.1057/9781137569943.0004

counterweights to the costs encountered in the activity. That is, every serious pursuit contains its own combination of tensions, dislikes, and disappointments, which each participant must confront in some way. For instance, an amateur football player may not always like attending daily practices, being bested occasionally by more junior players when there, and being required to sit on the sidelines from time to time while others get experience at his position. Yet he may still regard this activity as highly fulfilling – as (serious) leisure – because it also offers certain powerful rewards.

Put more precisely, then, the drive to find fulfillment in a serious pursuit is the drive to experience the rewards of a given work or leisure activity, such that its costs are seen by the participant as more or less insignificant by comparison. This is at once the meaning of the activity for the participant and that person's motivation for engaging in it. It is this motivational sense of the concept of reward that distinguishes it from the idea of durable benefit set out earlier, a concept that, as I said, emphasizes outcomes rather than antecedent conditions. Nonetheless, the two ideas constitute two sides of the same social psychological coin.

The rewards of a serious pursuit are the more or less routine values that attract and hold its enthusiasts. The careers in such pursuits both frame and are framed by the continuous search for these rewards, a search that takes months, and in some fields years, before the enthusiasts consistently find deep satisfaction in their amateur, hobbyist, or volunteer activity. Ten rewards have so far emerged in the course of the various exploratory studies of amateurs, hobbyists, and career volunteers. As the following list shows, the rewards are predominantly personal.

Personal rewards

1. Personal enrichment (cherished experiences)
2. Self-actualization (developing skills, abilities, knowledge)
3. Self-expression (expressing skills, abilities, knowledge already developed)
4. Self-image (known to others as a particular kind of serious leisure participant)
5. Self-gratification (combination of superficial enjoyment and deep fulfillment)

DOI: 10.1057/9781137569943.0004

6 Re-creation (regeneration) of oneself through serious leisure after a day's work
7 Financial return (from a serious leisure activity)

Social rewards

8 Social attraction (associating with other serious leisure participants, with clients as a volunteer, participating in the social world of the activity)
9 Group accomplishment (group effort in accomplishing a serious leisure project; senses of helping, being needed, being altruistic)
10 Contribution to the maintenance and development of the group (including senses of helping, being needed, being altruistic in making the contribution)

This brief discussion shows that some positive psychological states may be founded, to some extent, on particular negative (even infamous) conditions (e.g., tennis elbow, frostbite [cross-country skiing], stage fright, and frustration [in acquiring a collectable, learning a part]). Such conditions can make the senses of achievement and self-fulfillment even more pronounced as the enthusiast manages to conquer adversity. The broader lesson here is that, to understand motivation in serious leisure, we must always examine costs and rewards in their relationship to each other.

Serious leisure experiences also have a negative side, which must always be assessed. Accordingly I have always asked my respondents to discuss the costs they face in their serious leisure. But so far, it has been impossible to develop a general list of them, as has been done for rewards, since the costs tend to be highly specific to each serious leisure activity. Thus each activity I have studied to date has been found to have its own constellation of costs, but as the respondents see them, they are invariably and heavily outweighed in importance by the rewards of the activity. In general terms the costs discovered to date may be classified as disappointments, dislikes, or tensions. Nonetheless, all research on serious leisure considered, its costs are not nearly as commonly examined as its rewards, leaving thus a gap in our understanding that must be filled.

The costs of leisure may also be seen as one type of leisure constraint. Leisure constraints are "factors that limit people's participation in leisure

DOI: 10.1057/9781137569943.0004

activities, use of services, and satisfaction or enjoyment of current activities" (Scott, 2003, p. 75). Costs certainly dilute the satisfaction or enjoyment participants experience in pursuing certain leisure activities, even if, in their interpretation of them, those participants find such costs, or constraints, overridden by the powerful rewards also found there.

Thrills and flow

Thrills are part of this reward system. *Thrills*, or high points, are the sharply exciting events and occasions that stand out in the minds of those who pursue a kind of serious leisure or devotee work. In general, they tend to be associated with the rewards of self-enrichment and, to a lesser extent, those of self-actualization and self-expression. That is, thrills in serious leisure and devotee work may be seen as situated manifestations of certain more abstract rewards; they are what participants in some fields seek as concrete expressions of the rewards they find there. They are important, in substantial part, because they motivate the participant to stick with the pursuit in hope of finding similar experiences again and again and because they demonstrate that diligence and commitment may pay off. Because thrills, as defined here, are based on a certain level of mastery of a core activity, they know no equivalent in casual leisure. The thrill of a roller coaster ride is qualitatively different from a successful descent down a roaring rapid in a kayak where the boater has the experience, knowledge, and skill to accomplish this.

Over the years I have identified a number of thrills that come with the serious leisure activities I studied. These thrills are exceptional instances of the *flow* experience. Thus, although the idea of flow originated with the work of Mihalyi Csikszentmihalyi (1990), and has therefore an intellectual history quite separate from that of serious leisure, it does nevertheless happen, depending on the activity, that it is a key motivational force there (Stebbins, 2010). What then is flow?

The intensity with which some participants approach their leisure suggests that, there, they may at times be in psychological flow. Flow, a form of optimal experience, is possibly the most widely discussed and studied generic intrinsic reward in the psychology of work and leisure. Although many types of work and leisure generate little or no flow for their participants, those that do are found primarily in the serious pursuits of devotee work and serious leisure. Still it appears that each serious pursuit capable of producing flow does so in terms unique to it. And it follows that each of these activities, especially their core activities, must be carefully studied to discover the properties contributing to the distinctive flow experience it offers.

In his theory of optimal experience, Csikszentmihalyi (1990, pp. 3–5, 54) describes and explains the psychological foundation of the many flow activities in work and leisure, as exemplified in chess, dancing, surgery, and rock climbing. Flow is "autotelic" experience, or the sensation that comes with the actual enacting of intrinsically rewarding activity. Over the years Csikszentmihalyi (1990, pp. 49–67) has identified and explored eight components of this experience. It is easy to see how this quality of complex core activity, when present, is sufficiently rewarding and, it follows, highly valued to endow it with many of the qualities of serious leisure, thereby rendering the two, at the motivational level, inseparable in several ways. And this holds even though most people tend to think of work and leisure as vastly different. The eight components are

1 sense of competence in executing the activity;
2 requirement of concentration;
3 clarity of goals of the activity;
4 immediate feedback from the activity;
5 sense of deep, focused involvement in the activity;
6 sense of control in completing the activity;
7 loss of self-consciousness during the activity;
8 sense of time that is truncated during the activity.

These components are self-evident, except possibly for the first and the sixth. With reference to the first, flow fails to develop when the activity is either too easy or too difficult; to experience flow the participant must feel capable of performing a moderately challenging activity. The sixth component refers to the perceived degree of control the participant has over execution of the activity. This is not a matter of personal competence; rather it is one of degree of maneuverability in the fact of uncontrollable external forces, a condition well illustrated in situations faced by the mountain hobbyists mentioned above, as when the water level suddenly rises on the river or an unpredicted snowstorm results in a whiteout on a mountain snowboard slope.

Viewed from the SLP, psychological flow tends to be associated with the rewards of self-enrichment and, to a lesser extent, those of self-actualization and self-expression. Also to be considered part of the Perspective

DOI: 10.1057/9781137569943.0004

as well as part of flow theory are the pre- and post-flow phases of flow, recently examined by Elkington (2010).

Costs, uncontrollability, and marginality

From the earlier statement about costs and rewards, it is evident why the desire to participate in the core amateur, hobbyist, or volunteer activity can become for some participants some of the time significantly *uncontrollable*. This is because it engenders in its practitioners the desire to engage in the activity beyond the time or the money (if not both) available for it. As a professional violinist once counseled his daughter, "Rachel, never marry an amateur violinist! He will want to play quartets all night" (from Bowen, 1935, p. 93). There seems to be an almost universal desire to upgrade: to own a better set of golf clubs, buy a more powerful telescope, take more dance lessons perhaps from a renowned (and consequently more expensive) professional, and so forth. The same applies to hobbyist and volunteer pursuits.

Chances are therefore good that some serious leisure enthusiasts will be eager to spend more time at and money on the core activity than is likely to be countenanced by certain significant others who also make demands on that time and money. The latter may soon come to the interpretation that the enthusiast is more enamored of the core leisure activity than of, say, the partner or spouse. Charges of selfishness may, then, not be long off. I found in my research on serious leisure that attractive activity and selfishness are natural partners (Stebbins, 2007/2015, pp. 74–75). Whereas some casual leisure and even project-based leisure can also be uncontrollable, the marginality hypothesis (stated below) implies that such a proclivity is generally significantly stronger among serious leisure participants.

Uncontrollable or not serious leisure activities, given their intense appeal, can also be viewed as behavioral expressions of the participants' *central life interests* in those activities. In his book by the same title, Robert Dubin (1992) defines this interest as "that portion of a person's total life in which energies are invested in both physical/intellectual activities and in positive emotional states." Sociologically, a central life interest is often associated with a major role in life. And since they can only emerge from positive emotional states, obsessive and compulsive activities can never become central life interests.

DOI: 10.1057/9781137569943.0004

Finally, I have argued over the years that amateurs, and sometimes even the activities they pursue, are marginal in society, for amateurs are neither dabblers (casual leisure) nor professionals (see Stebbins, 2007/2015, p. 18). Moreover, studies of hobbyists and career volunteers show that they and some of their activities are just as marginal and for many of the same reasons. Several properties of serious leisure give substance to these observations. One, although seemingly illogical according to common sense, serious leisure is characterized empirically by an important degree of positive commitment to a pursuit. This commitment is measured, among other ways, by the sizeable investments of time and energy in the leisure made by its devotees and participants. Two, serious leisure is pursued with noticeable intentness, with such passion that Erving Goffman (1963, pp. 144–145) once branded amateurs and hobbyists as the "quietly disaffiliated." People with such orientations toward their leisure are marginal compared with people who go in for the ever-popular forms of much of casual leisure.

Career

Leisure career, introduced earlier as a central component of the definition of serious leisure and as one of its six distinguishing qualities, is important enough as a concept in this exposition of the basics of this form of leisure to warrant still further discussion. One reason for this special treatment is that a person's sense of the unfolding of his or her career in any complex role, leisure roles included, can be, at times, a powerful motive to act there. For example, a woman who knits a sweater that a friend praises highly is likely to feel some sense of her own abilities in this hobby and be motivated to continue in it, possibly trying more complicated patterns. Athletes who win awards for excellence in their sport can get from this a similar jolt of enthusiasm for participation there.

Exploratory research on careers in serious leisure has so far proceeded from a broad, rather loose definition: a leisure career is the typical course, or passage, of a type of amateur, hobbyist, or volunteer that carries the person into and through a leisure role and possibly into and through a work role. The essence of any career, whether in work, leisure, or elsewhere, lies in the temporal continuity of the activities associated with it. Moreover, we are accustomed to thinking of this continuity as one of

DOI: 10.1057/9781137569943.0004

accumulating rewards and prestige, as progress along these lines from some starting point, even though continuity may also include career retrogression. In the worlds of sport and entertainment, for instance, athletes and artists may reach performance peaks early on, after which the prestige and rewards diminish as the limelight shifts to younger, sometimes more capable practitioners. A detailed explanation of the leisure/devotee work career and the parallel leisure involvement scale is now available in Stebbins (2014).

Devotee work

The subject of devotee work and occupational devotion was briefly outlined in the Introduction. There it was observed that occupational devotees feel a powerful devotion, or strong, positive attachment, to a form of self-enhancing work. In such work the sense of achievement is high and the core activity endowed with such intense appeal that the line between this work and leisure is virtually erased. Further, it is by way of the core activity of their work that devotees realize a unique combination of, what are for them, strongly seated cultural values (Williams, 2000, p. 146): success, achievement, freedom of action, individual personality, and activity (being involved in something). Other categories of workers may also be animated by some, even all, of these values, but fail for various reasons to realize them in gainful employment.

Occupational devotees turn up chiefly, though not exclusively, in four areas of the economy, provided their work there is, at most, only lightly bureaucratized: certain small businesses, the skilled trades, the consulting and counseling occupations, and the public- and client-centered professions. Public-centered professions are found in the arts, sports, scientific, and entertainment fields, while those that are client-centered abound in such fields as law, teaching, accounting, and medicine (Stebbins, 1992, p. 22). It is assumed in all this that the work and its core activity to which people become devoted carries with it a respectable personal and social identity within their reference groups, since it would be difficult, if not impossible, to be devoted to work that those groups regarded with scorn. Still, positive identification with the job is not a defining condition of occupational devotion, since such identification can develop for other reasons, including high salary, prestigious employer, and advanced educational qualifications.

DOI: 10.1057/9781137569943.0004

The fact of devotee work for some people and its possibility for others signals that work, as one of life's domains, may be highly positive. Granted, most workers are not fortunate enough to find such work. For those who do find it, the work meets six criteria (Stebbins, 2004/2014, p. 9). To generate occupational devotion:

1 The valued core activity must be profound; to perform it acceptably requires substantial skill, knowledge, or experience or a combination of two or three of these.
2 The core must offer significant variety.
3 The core must also offer significant opportunity for creative or innovative work, as a valued expression of individual personality. The adjectives "creative" and "innovative" stress that the undertaking results in something new or different, showing imagination and application of routine skill or knowledge. That is, boredom is likely to develop only after the onset of fatigue experienced from long hours on the job, a point at which significant creativity and innovation are no longer possible.
4 The would-be devotee must have reasonable control over the amount and disposition of time put into the occupation (the value of freedom of action), such that he can prevent it from becoming a burden. Medium and large bureaucracies have tended to subvert this criterion. For, in interest of the survival and development of their organization, managers have felt they must deny their nonunionized employees this freedom, and force them to accept stiff deadlines and heavy workloads. But no activity, be it leisure or work, is so appealing that it invites unlimited participation during all waking hours.
5 The would-be devotee must have both an aptitude and a taste for the work in question. This is, in part, a case of one man's meat being another man's poison. John finds great fulfillment in being a physician, an occupation that holds little appeal for Jane who, instead, adores being a lawyer (work John finds unappealing).
6 The devotees must work in a physical and social milieu that encourages them to pursue often and without significant constraint the core activity. This includes avoidance of excessive paperwork, caseloads, class sizes, market demands, and the like.

Sounds ideal, if not idealistic, but in fact occupations and work roles exist that meet these criteria. In today's climate of occupational deskilling,

DOI: 10.1057/9781137569943.0004

overbureaucratization, and similar impediments to fulfilling core activity at work, many people find it difficult to locate or arrange devotee employment. The six criteria just listed also characterize serious leisure, giving further substance to the claim put forward here that such leisure and devotee work occupy a great deal of common ground. Together they constitute the class of serious pursuits.

Casual leisure

Casual leisure is immediately intrinsically rewarding, relatively short-lived pleasurable activity requiring little or no special training to enjoy it. It is fundamentally hedonic, pursued for its significant level of pure enjoyment, or pleasure. The term was coined by the author in the first conceptual statement about serious leisure (Stebbins, 1982), which at the time, depicted its casual counterpart as all activity not classifiable as serious (project-based leisure has since been added as a third form, see next section). Casual leisure is considerably less substantial than serious leisure, and offers no career of the sort found in the latter.

Its types – there are eight (see figure 1.1) – include *play* (including dabbling), *relaxation* (e.g., sitting, napping, strolling), *passive entertainment* (e.g., popular TV, books, recorded music), *active entertainment* (e.g., games of chance, party games), *sociable conversation* (e.g., gossiping, joking, talking about the weather), *sensory stimulation* (e.g., sex, eating, drinking, sight-seeing), and *casual volunteering* (as opposed to serious leisure, or career, volunteering). Casual volunteering includes handing out leaflets, stuffing envelopes, and collecting money door-to-door. Note that dabbling (as play) may occur in the same genre of activity pursued by amateurs, hobbyists, and career volunteers. The preceding section was designed, in part, to conceptually separate dabblers from this trio of leisure participants, thereby enabling the reader to interpret with sophistication references to, for example, "amateurish" activity (e.g., *The cult of the amateur* by Andrew Keen, 2007).

The last and newest type of casual leisure – *pleasurable aerobic activity* – refers to physical activities that require effort sufficient to cause marked increase in respiration and heart rate. As applied here the term "aerobic activity" is broad in scope, encompassing all activity that calls for such effort, which, to be sure, includes the routines pursued collectively in (narrowly conceived of) aerobics classes and those pursued individually

DOI: 10.1057/9781137569943.0004

by way of televised or videotaped programs of aerobics (Stebbins, 2004). Yet, as with its passive and active cousins in entertainment, pleasurable aerobic activity is basically casual leisure. That is, to do such activity requires little more than minimal skill, knowledge, or experience. Examples include the game of the Hash House Harriers (a type of treasure hunt in the outdoors), kickball (described in *The Economist*, 2005, as a cross between soccer and baseball), "exergames" for children (a video game played on a dance floor; Gerson, 2010), and such children's pastimes as hide-and-seek.

People seem to pursue the different types of casual leisure in combinations of two and three at least as often as they pursue them separately. For instance, every type can be relaxing, producing in this fashion play-relaxation, passive entertainment-relaxation, and so on. Various combinations of play and sensory stimulation are also possible, as in experimenting, in deviant or nondeviant ways, with drug use, sexual activity, and thrill seeking through movement. Additionally, sociable conversation accompanies some sessions of sensory stimulation (e.g., recreational drug use, curiosity seeking, displays of beauty) as well as some sessions of relaxation and active and passive entertainment, although such conversation normally tends to be rather truncated in the latter two.

This brief review of the types of casual leisure reveals that they share at least one central property: all are hedonic. More precisely, all produce a significant level of pure pleasure, or enjoyment, for those participating in them. In broad, colloquial language, casual leisure could serve as the scientific term for the practice of doing what comes naturally. Yet, paradoxically, this leisure is by no means wholly frivolous, for we shall see shortly that some clear benefits come from pursuing it. Moreover, unlike the evanescent hedonic property of casual leisure itself, its benefits are enduring, a property that makes them worthy of extended analysis in their own right.

It follows that terms such as "pleasure" and "enjoyment" are the more appropriate descriptors of the rewards of casual leisure in contrast to terms such as "fulfillment" and "rewardingness," which best describe the rewards gained in serious leisure. At least the serious leisure participants interviewed by the author were inclined to describe their involvements as fulfilling or rewarding rather than pleasurable or enjoyable. Still, overlap exists, for both casual and serious leisure offer the hedonic reward of self-gratification (see reward number 5). The activity is fun to do, even

DOI: 10.1057/9781137569943.0004

if the fun component is considerably more prominent in casual leisure than in its serious counterpart.

Notwithstanding its hedonic nature casual leisure is by no means wholly inconsequential, for some clear costs and benefits accrue from pursuing it. Moreover, in contrast to the evanescent hedonic property of casual leisure itself, these costs and benefits are enduring. The benefits include serendipitous creativity and discovery in play, regeneration from earlier intense activity, and development and maintenance of interpersonal relationships (Stebbins, 2007/2015, pp. 41–43). Some of its costs root in excessive casual leisure or lack of variety as manifested in boredom or lack of time for leisure activities that contribute to self through acquisition of skills, knowledge, and experience (i.e., serious leisure). Moreover, casual leisure is alone unlikely to produce a distinctive leisure identity.

Moreover, my own observations of casual leisure suggest that hedonism, or self-gratification, although it is a principal reward here, must still share the stage with one or two other rewards. Thus any type of casual leisure, like any type of serious leisure, can also help *recreate*, or regenerate, its participants following a lengthy stint of obligatory activity. Furthermore, some forms of casual and serious leisure offer the reward of *social attraction*, the appeal of being with other people while participating in a common activity. Nevertheless, even though some casual and serious leisure participants share certain rewards, research on this question will likely show that these two types experience them in sharply different ways. For example, the social attraction of belonging to a barbershop chorus or a company of actors with all its specialized shoptalk diverges considerably from that of belonging to a group of people playing a party game or taking a boat tour where such talk is highly unlikely to occur.

Benefits of casual leisure

We have so far been able to identify five benefits, or outcomes, of casual leisure. But since this is a preliminary list – it is first attempt at making one – it is certainly possible that future research and theorizing could add to it.

One lasting benefit of casual leisure is the creativity and discovery it sometimes engenders. Serendipity, "the quintessential form of informal experimentation, accidental discovery, and spontaneous invention"

DOI: 10.1057/9781137569943.0004

(Stebbins, 2001b), usually underlies these two processes, suggesting that serendipity and casual leisure are at times closely aligned. In casual leisure, as elsewhere, serendipity can lead to highly varied results, including a new understanding of a home gadget or government policy, a sudden realization that a particular plant or bird exists in the neighborhood, or a different way of making artistic sounds on a musical instrument. Such creativity or discovery is unintended, however, and is therefore accidental. Moreover, it is not ordinarily the result of a problem-solving orientation of people taking part in casual leisure, since most of the time at least they have little interest in trying to solve problems while engaging in this kind of activity. Usually problems for which solutions must be found emerge at work, while meeting nonwork obligations, or during serious leisure.

Another benefit springs from what Chris Daniels labeled in 1975 *edutainment* (*New World Encyclopedia*, 2008), which holds that this benefit of casual leisure comes with participating in such mass entertainment as watching films and television programs, listening to popular music, and reading popular books and articles. Theme parks and museums are also considered sources of edutainment. While consuming media or frequenting places of this sort, these participants inadvertently learn something of substance about the social and physical world in which they live. They are, in a word, entertained and educated in the same breath.

Third, casual leisure affords regeneration, or re-creation, possibly even more so than its counterpart, serious leisure, since the latter can sometimes be intense. Of course, many a leisure studies specialist has observed that leisure in general affords relaxation or entertainment, if not both, and that these constitute two of its principal benefits. What is new, then, in the observation just made is that it distinguishes between casual and serious leisure, and more importantly, that it emphasizes the enduring effects of relaxation and entertainment when they help enhance overall equanimity, most notably in the interstices between periods of intense activity.

A fourth benefit that may flow from participation in casual leisure originates in the development and maintenance of interpersonal relationships. One of its types, the sociable conversation, is particularly fecund in this regard, but other types, when shared, as sometimes happens during sensory stimulation and passive and active entertainment, can also have the same effect. The interpersonal relationships in question are many and varied, and encompass those that form between friends, spouses, and

DOI: 10.1057/9781137569943.0004

members of families. Such relationships, Hutchinson and Kleiber (2005) found in a set of studies of some of the benefits of casual leisure, can foster personal psychological growth by promoting new shared interests and, in the course of this process, new positive appraisals of self.

Well-being is still another benefit that can flow from engaging in casual leisure. Speaking only for the realm of leisure, perhaps the greatest sense of well-being is achieved when a person develops an *optimal leisure lifestyle*. Such a lifestyle is "the deeply satisfying pursuit during free time of one or more substantial, absorbing forms of serious leisure, complemented by a judicious amount of casual leisure" (Stebbins, 2007/2015). People find optimal leisure lifestyles by partaking of leisure activities that individually and in combination realize human potential and enhance quality of life and well-being. Project-based leisure can also enhance a person's leisure lifestyle. The study of kayakers, snowboarders, and mountain and ice climbers (Stebbins, 2005b) revealed that the vast majority of the three samples used various forms of casual leisure to optimally round out their use of free time. For them their serious leisure was a central life interest, but their casual leisure contributed to overall well-being by allowing for relaxation, regeneration, sociability, entertainment, and other activities less intense than their serious leisure.

Still well-being experienced during free time is more than this, as Hutchinson and Kleiber (2005) observed, since this kind of leisure can contribute to self-protection, as by buffering stress and sustaining coping efforts. Casual leisure can also preserve or restore a sense of self. This was sometimes achieved in their samples, when subjects said they rediscovered in casual leisure fundamental personal or familial values or a view of themselves as caring people.

Project-based leisure

Project-based leisure (Stebbins, 2005a) is the third form of leisure activity and the most recent one added to the Perspective. It is a short-term, reasonably complicated, one-off or occasional, though infrequent, creative undertaking carried out in free time, or time free of disagreeable obligation. Such leisure requires considerable planning, effort, and sometimes skill or knowledge, but is for all that neither serious leisure nor intended to develop into such. The adjective "occasional" describes widely spaced undertakings for such regular occasions as religious festivals, someone's birthday, or a national holiday. Volunteering for a sports event may be seen as an occasional project. The adjective "creative" stresses that the undertaking results in something new or different, by showing imagination and perhaps routine skill or knowledge. Though most projects would appear to be continuously pursued until completed, it is conceivable that some might be interrupted for several weeks, months, even years (e.g., a stone wall in the back garden that gets finished only after its builder recovers from an operation on his strained back). Only when a rudimentary social world springs up around the project, it does, in its own particular way, bring together friends, neighbors, or relatives (e.g., through a genealogical project or Christmas celebrations), or draw the individual participant into an organizational milieu (e.g., through volunteering for a sports event or major convention).

Moreover, it appears that, in some instances, project-based leisure springs from a sense of obligation to undertake it. If so, it is nonetheless, as leisure, uncoerced activity, in the sense that the obligation is in fact "agreeable" – the project creator in executing the project anticipates finding fulfillment, obligated to do so or not. And worth exploring in future research, given that some obligations can be pleasant and attractive, is the nature and extent of leisure-like projects carried out within the context of paid employment. Furthermore, this discussion jibes with the additional criterion that the project, to qualify as project-based leisure, must be *seen by the project creator* as fundamentally uncoerced, fulfilling activity. Finally, note that project-based leisure cannot, by definition, refer to projects executed as part of a person's serious leisure, such as mounting a star night as an amateur astronomer or a model train display as a collector.

Though not serious leisure, project-based leisure is enough like it to justify using the SLP to develop a parallel framework for exploring this neglected class of activities. A main difference is that project-based leisure fails to generate a sense of career. Otherwise, however, there is here need to persevere, some skill or knowledge may be required, and, invariably, effort is called for. Also present are recognizable benefits, a special identity, and often a social world of sorts, though it appears, one usually less complicated than those surrounding many serious leisure activities. And perhaps it happens at times that, even if not intended at the moment as participation in a type of serious leisure, the skilled, artistic, or intellectual aspects of the project prove so attractive that the participant decides, after the fact, to make a leisure career of their pursuit as a hobby or an amateur activity.

DOI: 10.1057/9781137569943.0004

Project-based leisure is also capable of generating many of the rewards experienced in serious leisure. And, as in serious leisure so in project-based leisure: these rewards constitute part of the motivational basis for pursuing such highly fulfilling activity. Furthermore, motivation to undertake a leisure project may have an organizational base, much as many other forms of leisure do (Stebbins, 2002). My observations suggest that small groups, grassroots associations (volunteer groups with few or no paid staff), and volunteer organizations (paid-staff groups using volunteer help) are the most common types of organizations in which people undertake project-based leisure.

Motivationally speaking, project-based leisure may be attractive in substantial part because it does not demand long-term commitment, as serious leisure does. Even occasional projects carry with them the sense that the undertaking in question has a definite end and may even be terminated prematurely. Thus project-based leisure is no central life interest (Dubin, 1992). Rather it is viewed by participants as fulfilling (as distinguished from enjoyable or hedonic) activity that can be experienced comparatively quickly, though certainly not as quickly as casual leisure.

Project-based leisure fits into leisure lifestyle in its own peculiar way as interstitial activity, like some casual leisure but not like most serious leisure. It can therefore help shape a person's optimal leisure lifestyle. For instance, it can usually be pursued at times convenient for the participant. It follows that project-based leisure is nicely suited to people who, out of proclivity or extensive nonleisure obligations or both, reject serious leisure and, yet, who also have no appetite for a steady diet of casual leisure. Among the candidates for project-based leisure are people with heavy workloads; homemakers, mothers, and fathers with extensive domestic responsibilities; unemployed individuals who, though looking for work, still have time at the moment for (I suspect, mostly one-shot) projects; and avid serious leisure enthusiasts who want a temporary change in their leisure lifestyle. Retired people, who often do have time for plenty of free time, may find project-based leisure attractive as a way to add variety to their lifestyle. Beyond these special categories of participant, project-based leisure offers a form of substantial leisure to all adults, adolescents, and even children looking for something interesting and exciting to do in free time that is neither casual nor serious leisure.

DOI: 10.1057/9781137569943.0004

Although, at most, only a rudimentary social world springs up around a project, it can in its own particular way bring together friends, neighbors, or relatives (e.g., through a genealogical project), or draw the individual participant into an organizational milieu (e.g., through volunteering for a sports event). This further suggests that project-based leisure often has, in at least two ways, potential for building community. One, it can bring into contact people who otherwise have no reason to meet, or at least meet frequently. Two, by way of event volunteering and other collective altruistic activity, it can contribute to carrying off community events and projects. Project-based leisure is not, however, civil labor, which must be classified as exclusively serious leisure (Rojek, 2002).

Types of project-based leisure

It was noted in the definition just presented that project-based leisure is not all the same. Whereas systematic exploration may reveal others, two types are evident at this time: one-shot projects and occasional projects. These are presented next using the classificatory framework for amateur, hobbyist, and volunteer activities developed earlier in this chapter.

One-shot projects

In all these projects people generally use the talents and knowledge they have at hand, even though for some projects they may seek certain instructions beforehand, including reading a book or taking a short course. And some projects resembling hobbyist activity participation may require a modicum of preliminary conditioning. Always, the goal is to undertake successfully the one-off project and nothing more, and sometimes a small amount of background preparation is necessary for this. It is possible that a survey would show that most project-based leisure is hobbyist in character and the next most common, a kind of volunteering. First, the following hobbyist-like projects have so far been identified:

- Making and tinkering:
  - Interlacing, interlocking, and knot-making from kits

DOI: 10.1057/9781137569943.0004

    - Other kit assembly projects (e.g., stereo tuner, craft store projects)
    - Do-it-yourself projects done primarily for fulfillment, some of which may even be undertaken with minimal skill and knowledge (e.g., build a rock wall or a fence, finish a room in the basement, plant a special garden). This could turn into an irregular series of such projects, spread over many years, possibly even transforming the participant into a hobbyist.
- Liberal arts:
    - Genealogy (not as ongoing hobby)
    - Tourism: special trip, not as part of an extensive personal tour program, to visit different parts of a region, a continent, or much of the world.
- Activity participation: long back-packing trip, canoe trip; one-off mountain ascent (e.g., Fuji, Rainier, Kilimanjaro).

One-off volunteering projects are also common, though possibly somewhat less so than hobbyist-like projects. And less common than either are the amateur-like projects, which seem to concentrate in the sphere of theater.

- Volunteering
    - Volunteer at a convention or conference, whether local, national, or international in scope.
    - Volunteer at a sporting competition, whether local, national, or international in scope.
    - Volunteer at an arts festival or special exhibition mounted in a museum.
    - Volunteer to help restore human life or wildlife after a natural or human-made disaster caused by, for instance, a hurricane, earthquake, oil spill, or industrial accident.
- Arts projects (this new category replaces Entertainment Theater, see Stebbins, 2011):
    - Entertainment theater: produce a skit or one-off community pageant; prepare a home film, video or set of photos.
    - Public speaking: prepare a talk for a reunion, an after-dinner speech, an oral position statement on an issue to be discussed at a community meeting.
    - Memoirs: therapeutic audio, visual, and written productions by the elderly; life histories and autobiographies (all ages); accounts of personal events (all ages) (Stebbins, 2011).

DOI: 10.1057/9781137569943.0004

Occasional projects

The occasional projects seem more likely to originate in or be motivated by agreeable obligation than their one-off cousins. Examples of occasional projects include the sum of the culinary, decorative, or other creative activities undertaken, for example, at home or at work for a religious occasion or someone's birthday. Likewise, national holidays and similar celebrations sometimes inspire individuals to mount occasional projects consisting of an ensemble of inventive elements.

Unlike one-off projects occasional projects have the potential to become routinized, which happens when new creative possibilities no longer come to mind as the participant arrives at a fulfilling formula wanting no further modification. North Americans who decorate their homes the same way each Christmas season exemplify this situation. Indeed, it can happen that, over the years, such projects may lose their appeal, but not their necessity, thereby becoming disagreeable obligations, which their authors no longer define as leisure.

And, lest it be overlooked, note that one-off projects also hold the possibility of becoming unpleasant. Thus, the hobbyist genealogist gets overwhelmed with the details of family history and the challenge of verifying dates. The thought of putting in time and effort doing something once considered leisure but which she now dislikes makes no sense. Likewise, volunteering for a project may turn sour, creating in the volunteer a sense of being faced with a disagreeable obligation, which however, must still be honored. This is leisure no more.

Conclusion

The SLP is both individual and contextual in scope. Looking closely at the individual component, it is possible to discern another first principle, namely, that leisure is what a person does in free time. People, when they think about free time, also think about what they do during it and what that means to them. If asked they can give a list of the general activities pursued here. They can also evaluate these activities as, say, intensely interesting (a serious leisure passion), as moderately interesting (e.g., a leisure project), or as not very interesting (a common complaint about some television programming). Furthermore they can speak about their past leisure activities and the one's they would like to take up in the future.

DOI: 10.1057/9781137569943.0004

This seventh principle is primarily descriptive – what one does – whereas the sixth principle on leisure's role in achieving work/life balance, is utilitarian. Here leisure is conceived of as useful (immensely so) in finding an agreeable equilibrium for all of life's everyday activities. The eighth principle – the unique image by which leisure is known in the larger world – is examined in the next chapter. This principle is cultural, in that it expresses the collective, or communal, view of leisure.

References

Arai, S.M., & Pedlar, A.M. (1997). Building Communities through leisure: Citizen participation in a healthy communities initiative. *Journal of Leisure Research*, 29, 167–182.

Bowen, C.D. (1935). *Friends and fiddlers.* Boston, MA: Little Brown.

Csikszentmihalyi, M. (1990). *Flow: The psychology of optimal experience.* New York: Harper & Row.

Davidson, L., & Stebbins, R.A. (2011). *Serious leisure and nature: Sustainable consumption in the outdoors.* Houndmills, Basingstoke, UK: Palgrave Macmillan.

Dubin, R. (1992). *Central life interests: Creative individualism in a complex world.* New Brunswick, NJ: Transaction.

The Economist (2005). Up off the couch. October 22, p. 35.

Elkington, S. (2010). Articulating a systematic phenomenology of flow: An experience-process perspective. *Leisure/Loisir*, 34, 327–360.

Gerson, J. (2010). Video games keep kids fit. *Calgary Herald*, Wednesday, December 8, B1.

Goffman, E. (1963). *Stigma: Notes on the management of spoiled identity.* Englewood Cliffs, NJ: Prentice-Hall.

Hutchinson, S.L., & Kleiber, D.A. (2005). Gifts of the ordinary: Casual leisure's contributions to health and well-being. *World Leisure Journal*, 47(3), 2–16.

New World Encyclopedia (2008). Edutainment. (http://www.newworldencyclopedia.org/entry/Edutainment, retrieved March 3, 2012).

Rojek, C. (2002). Civil labour, leisure and post work society. *Société et Loisir/Society and Leisure*, 25, 21–36.

Scott, D. (2003). Constraints. In J.M. Jenkins & J.J. Pigram (Eds.), *Encyclopedia of leisure and outdoor recreation* (pp. 75–78). London: Routledge.

DOI: 10.1057/9781137569943.0004

Siegenthaler, K.L., & O'Dell, I. (2003). Older golfers: Serious leisure and successful aging. *World Leisure Journal*, 45(1), 45–52.
Stebbins, R.A. (1982). Serious leisure: A conceptual statement. *Pacific Sociological Review*, 25, 251–272.
Stebbins, R.A. (1992). *Amateurs, professionals, and serious leisure.* Montreal, QC and Kingston, ON: McGill-Queen's University Press.
Stebbins, R.A. (1994). The liberal arts hobbies: A neglected subtype of serious leisure. *Loisir et Société/Society and Leisure*, 16, 173–186.
Stebbins, R.A. (1996). Volunteering: A serious leisure perspective. *Nonprofit and Voluntary Action Quarterly*, 25, 211–224.
Stebbins, R.A. (2001). Volunteering – mainstream and marginal: Preserving the leisure experience. In M. Graham & M. Foley (Eds.), *Volunteering in leisure: Marginal or inclusive?* (Vol. 75, pp. 1–10). Eastbourne, UK: Leisure Studies Association.
Stebbins, R.A. (2001a). *New directions in the theory and research of serious leisure*, Mellen Studies in Sociology, Vol. 28. Lewiston, NY: Edwin Mellen.
Stebbins, R.A. (2001b). *Exploratory research in the social sciences.* Thousand Oaks, CA: Sage.
Stebbins, R.A. (2002). *The organizational basis of leisure participation: A motivational exploration.* State College, PA: Venture Publishing.
Stebbins, R.A. (2004/2014). *Between work and leisure: The common ground of two separate worlds.* New Brunswick, NJ: Transaction Publishers. (paperback edition with new Preface, 2014).
Stebbins, R.A. (2004). Pleasurable aerobic activity: A type of casual leisure with salubrious implications. *World Leisure Journal*, 46(4), 55–58 (also available at www.seriousleisure.net – Digital Library, Other Works).
Stebbins, R.A. (2005a). Project-based leisure: Theoretical neglect of a common use of free time. *Leisure Studies*, 24, 1–11.
Stebbins, R.A. (2005b). *Challenging mountain nature: Risk, motive, and lifestyle in three hobbyist sports*. Calgary, AB: Detselig.
Stebbins, R.A. (2007/2015). *Serious leisure: A perspective for our time.* New Brunswick, NJ: Transaction (paperback edition with new Preface, 2015).
Stebbins, R.A. (2010). Flow in serious leisure: Nature and prevalence, *Leisure Studies Association Newsletter*, No. 87 (November), pp. 21–23. Also available in the Digital Library at HYPERLINK "http://www.seriousleisure.net" www.seriousleisure.net.

Stebbins, R.A. (2011). "Personal Memoirs, Project-Based Leisure and Therapeutic Recreation for Seniors." *Leisure Studies Association Newsletter* 88, March (2011): 29–31. (also available at www.seriousleisure.net – Digital Library, "Leisure Reflections No. 26").
Stebbins, R.A. (2013). Unpaid work of love: Defining the work-leisure axis of volunteering. *Leisure Studies*, 32, 339–345.
Stebbins, R.A. (2014). *Careers in serious leisure: From dabbler to devotee in search of fulfillment.* Houndmills, UK: Palgrave Macmillan.
Unruh, D.R. (1979). Characteristics and types of participation in social worlds. *Symbolic Interaction*, 2, 115–130.
Unruh, D.R. (1980). The nature of social worlds. *Pacific Sociological Review*, 23, 271–296.
Williams, R.M., Jr. (2000). American society. In E.F. Borgatta, & R.J.V. Montgomery (Eds.), *Encyclopedia of sociology*, 2nd ed., Vol. 1 (pp. 140–148). New York: Macmillan.
Yoder, D.G. (1997). A model for commodity intensive serious leisure. *Journal of Leisure Research*, 29, 407–429.

DOI: 10.1057/9781137569943.0004

2

Positiveness in the Serious Pursuits

Abstract: *Three eudaemonic, positive processes and their outcomes, or products – self-efficacy, self-fulfillment, and identity development – are especially prominent in the serious pursuits. Additionally, a variety of positive emotions cluster around the serious pursuits, one of them being interest. Self-efficacy rests, in part, on self-directed learning and personal agency. Every serious pursuit is carried out within a social world, participation there being in general a richly positive experience. Positive leisure space may be institutional, temporal, or geographic. Serious leisure participants also develop a strong attachment to and identification with the geographic space in which they pursue their core activities. Some serious leisure participants also develop a strong attachment to and identification with the space in which they use their bodies to pursue their core activities. That is, body form or functioning, if not both, is seen as crucial and may become a condition of pride and fulfillment.*

Keywords: body; eudaemonia; identity; self-efficacy; self-fulfillment; serious pursuit; social world; space

Stebbins, Robert A. *Leisure and Positive Psychology: Linking Activities with Positiveness*. Basingstoke: Palgrave Macmillan, 2015. DOI: 10.1057/9781137569943.0005.

Three eudaemonic, positive processes and their outcomes, or products – self-efficacy, fulfillment, and identity development – are especially prominent in the serious pursuits. The three also fire some leisure projects, albeit by diminished degrees of each. Meanwhile, self-efficacy, self-fulfillment, and personal identity development are uncommon in the hedonic, casual leisure activities. Exceptions to this latter observation include meeting some of the challenges recorded in the Guinness World Records. Here a positive identity is established by way of a simple though remarkable achievement (e.g., Cohen-Gewerc & Stebbins, 2013, pp. 128–129).

After a discussion of the emotional side of the serious pursuits, this chapter moves to an examination of the above three processes. The social worlds of the serious pursuits, themselves repositories of positive arrangements and structures, are taken up next. The chapter continues with an extensive look at positive space, then terminating with a discussion of the positive body. We may expect all this and more when participants are magnetically drawn to a serious pursuit.

Emotion and the serious pursuits

A variety of positive emotions cluster around the serious pursuits. One of them is interest, served up in the serious pursuits as a person's "central life interests" (see Chapter 1). All the activities in serious leisure and devotee work are, emotionally speaking, central life interests. They also spawn the emotion of pride in what the participant has achieved and that of hope that achievement will occur. Further, achievement can contribute to the rise of self-confidence. Thus it is clear that the core activities at the center of the serious pursuits offer fertile ground in which positiveness can take root and grow.

Nonetheless, a complicating feature of the serious pursuits is that some of these positive emotions may not be experienced. Instead, their opposite may spring forth, such that pride turns to shame (e.g., forgetting one's lines while performing a play), hope to fear (e.g., that the critics will pan the writer's book), and confidence to timidity (e.g., because the meal was a flop, the hobbyist cook balks at attempting another). The characteristic of perseverance (see Chapter 1) helps the enthusiast over these momentary emotional hurdles, which nevertheless are poignant, memorable experiences. These emotions, both positive and negative, relate to the three positive processes.

DOI: 10.1057/9781137569943.0005

Self-efficacy

From the viewpoint of positive psychology, it is important to remember that self-efficacy (Bandura, 1997), fulfillment, and identity are manifested very differently in leisure, depending on the serious pursuit being considered. This holds even within major types and subtypes. For example, in the arts, efficacy is differently expressed in music compared with writing. Efficacious musicians believe they can master their musical instrument according to the standards of the type of music they are attracted to. They also believe they can learn to read music, perhaps even to sight read it well. On a third dimension of efficaciousness, they believe they can interpret acceptably the music they strive to play.

By contrast, efficacious writers believe in their ability to write such works as poems or novels. More particularly, they believe they can find the best words to express their ideas, conceive of imaginative plots (in their novels), and write works that will impress their peers and, possibly, a public. They also believe that they can create characters that will fit well in the plot in which they are set. Essayists believe in their capacity to shape and present a coherent literary treatment of a certain problem.

In the main, belief here refers to feeling competent to pursue in a fulfilling way particular core activities in serious leisure or devotee work. This belief in oneself is, in good measure, born of the (1) routine successes that accumulate with enduring, systematic pursuit of an activity, (2) encouragement from other people involved it, and (3) encouragement from noninvolved close associates of the participant such as parents, friends, and spouses. Additionally, since confidence is closely aligned with self-efficacy, it is noteworthy that leisure educators strive to instill both in their clients and students. Dattilo and Murphy (1991, pp. 147–152), for example, do this by encouraging participants in leisure to accept personal responsibility for their actions there. Leitner and Leitner (2004, pp. 313–314) first point out the need to overcome low self-esteem, then go on to show how people can accomplish this through engaging in "complex" (i.e., serious, project-based) leisure.

Self-directed learning and agency

A central process in the serious pursuits and one that also boosts self-efficacy there is self-directed learning (SDL). Roberson (2005, p. 205),

DOI: 10.1057/9781137569943.0005

drawing on an earlier conceptualization by Lambdin (1997), states that "self-directed learning is intentional and self-planned learning where the individual is clearly in control of this process." Such learning may be formal (here it would be synonymous with adult education), but most often it is informal. An important condition is that the learner controls the start, direction, and termination of the learning experience. Both adult education and SDL are types of "lifelong learning." The latter as an idea is broader than the first two, summarized by Selman and colleagues (1998, p. 21) as learning done throughout a person's lifetime, "from the cradle to the grave."

Self-efficacy rests on, among other conditions, knowledge about how to execute the core activities of the serious pursuit. For instance, musicians should have greater self-efficacy in playing their instrument to the extent that they have learned the techniques for doing this. Writers will have greater efficacy to the extent that they read some of the best exemplars of the genre of literature in which they are trying to excel.

Be that as it may, it is one thing to be self-efficacious and motivated to undertake the requisite SDL and quite another to organize life such that this actually happens. The serious pursuits are long-term endeavors, which give rise to leisure careers. Succeeding in them, even modestly, requires significant personal agency over the years, wherein the participant organizes, depending on the activity, regular sessions of learning, practice, writing, performing, and so forth. And participants must have not only considerable initiative and organizational talent but also considerable influence with those intimates who make occasional demands on their time. Thus, learning about jazz or classical music requires time for plenty of reading, as does learning how to write *belles lettres*. Would-be authors must learn well the stylistic conventions of their language as well as a vocabulary that will facilitate expression of their ideas.

Self-fulfillment

Self-fulfillment refers to either the act or the process of developing to the full one's capacity, or more particularly, to developing one's gifts and character. In this sense fulfillment and achievement are closely intertwined. It was observed earlier that the serious pursuits are highly fulfilling. Nevertheless, each serious activity has its own recipe for fulfillment. For instance, fulfillment is different in a team sport like basketball compared with an individual sport like long-distance running. In the former

DOI: 10.1057/9781137569943.0005

players may experience the rewards of participating in good teamwork and the camaraderie of collectively winning a game or, even more exciting, a tournament or championship. In the latter the participants are in it alone, mostly sharing their successes with interested nonparticipants (e.g., spouses, friends). Both types of sport offer further opportunities for fulfillment through acquisition of skill and knowledge. Here, the link to personal gifts and character becomes especially evident, as seen in athletes endowed with exceptional balance, speed, or strength.

An excursus on satisfaction and self-fulfillment

Both as researchers in the positive sciences and as participants in everyday life, we hear it all the time: "I sure had fun last night at the football game"; "It will be a fun time at Joan's sleepover"; "it was a most enjoyable evening" (said to the host). Much less often do we hear leisure experiences being described as satisfying or fulfilling, even if, for their participants, some experiences have precisely that quality. Why these differences in choice of descriptors for positive leisure experience, and what do these four descriptors mean in science and common sense (Stebbins, 2009, pp. 90–92)?

Common sense usage of the four, as typical of common sense everywhere, is rather loose and for the first two broadly applied. Thus the adjective "fun" usually denotes finding pleasure or amusement in a particular activity, while the adjective "enjoyable" typically refers to an activity that can be enjoyed, that gives pleasure or delight. In other words these two descriptors are basically synonyms. Turning to the third term, a satisfying experience, in one sense of the word, is itself synonymous with an experience that is fun or enjoyable (sometimes referred to as gratifying). But another sense of this adjective is substantially different: it refers to meeting or satisfying a need or want. Put otherwise a satisfying experience, in this second sense, leads to contentment with reference to a particular need or want, an additional meaning that sets it apart from the other three descriptors. By contrast, the fourth term, in one sense, points to a fulfilling experience, or more precisely, to a set of chronological experiences leading to development to the fullest of a person's gifts and character, to development of that person's full potential. A second sense of this adjective is, however, synonymous with the second sense of satisfying.

DOI: 10.1057/9781137569943.0005

These four descriptors form a rough scale of depth of leisure experience, running from that which is superficial – fun – to that which is profound – fulfillment. In common sense usage we seem, in crude fashion, to recognize these differences, in that, for example, few people would describe a sleepover as fulfilling or a grueling marathon as fun or enjoyable. The task of positive leisure science, and this section, is to recognize the existence of this implicit, common sense scale of leisure experience, while for scientific purposes, to try to iron out vagueness and inconsistency as these plague everyday usage of the four terms. We turn first to fun.

Because of the dual meaning of satisfaction, I have found it necessary, when striving to be as clear as possible about the rewards of serious leisure, to rely exclusively on the concept of fulfillment. It is substantially different from satisfaction, even in the second sense of the word. The serious pursuits are about satisfying achievement and accomplishment, of that there is no doubt, but it is also about personal development and self-confidence, of maximizing one's gifts and character through pursuit of particular leisure/devotee work activities (see Stebbins, 2004, 2014). Meanwhile, satisfaction can also mean becoming content or being content through gratification or pleasure experienced in an activity, which may well be of the casual leisure variety (see below).

To avoid this confusion when talking about the rewards of the serious pursuits, it has become necessary to frame discussion in the less ambiguous language of fulfillment rather than the more ambiguous language of satisfaction. The latter is a slippery concept, primarily because it is cursed with two quite different meanings. Moreover, experiencing achievement (the second meaning) is not really the same as experiencing fulfillment. For the latter rests on a clear sense of a "formative career" (Stebbins, 2009, pp. 68–69) in a complex role (found in work, leisure, a relationship, etc.), on the sense of realizing one's gifts and character over many years. Achievement, by contrast, results from a particular effort at a particular time in life. Thus fulfillment is, among several other things, a series of interrelated achievements interpreted by the achiever across a span of time.

Be that as it may, serious leisure enthusiasts do, at times, qualify their activities as fun. I have tried to deal with this seeming anomaly by invoking the idea of gratification (see list of rewards, Chapter 1). Over the years I have come to describe as gratifying an activity that the participant sees as fun, but that also generates fulfillment. For instance, some of the kayakers in the Canadian Rockies whom we interviewed and who possessed the appropriate skills and experience said it is "fun" to paddle Class-4 Rivers.

DOI: 10.1057/9781137569943.0005

By this they meant that the activity is gratifying, because with time, they have acquired the technical qualifications to carry it off with relative ease (Stebbins, 2005). This level of activity is fun, precisely because it is technically difficult but nonetheless quite manageable (it is fulfilling), given the participant's high level of development in the hobby.

In technical activities of this sort, fun has also been found to be a significant component of the flow experience, as seen in Csikszentmihalyi's (1990, pp. 49 and 72) linking of enjoyment with flow. But more recent thought on the matter by Seligman and Csikszentmihalyi (2000, p. 12) has led them to distinguish between the "pleasure" of what we have been calling fun (in casual leisure) from the "enjoyment" of activities referred to in this book as serious leisure. In their newer conceptualization enjoyment and self-fulfillment amount to the same thing.

Identity development

The serious pursuits are necessarily identity-generating endeavors. The special effort leading to a recognized level of achievement in an amateur, hobbyist, or career volunteer activity resonates with those who know the activity and respect what participants can do there. In their content, of course, these identities vary enormously. For instance, a volunteer docent at the local zoo known for her excellent teaching skills has a different image among her peers than a hobbyist philatelist renowned widely for his remarkable collection of nineteenth-century British stamps.

In short, a major part of what is positive about personal identity in a serious pursuit is nourished by in the activity itself, particularly its core. That identity is further enhanced by the fact that what is engaged in as a serious pursuit is done for, among other reasons, the love of it (in effect all amateurs, hobbyists, and career volunteers are *amators*). And devotee workers are *amators*, too, though they are also motivated, sometimes in convoluted ways, by the need for a livelihood (Stebbins, 2004/2014, chap. 6).

Social worlds

Every serious pursuit is carried out within a social world, although these formations vary in complexity according to the activity around which it

DOI: 10.1057/9781137569943.0005

has evolved. In general, the older the activity, the greater is its complexity. Consider parkour, or the hobby of rapidly negotiating (usually) urban natural and artificial obstacles using only the participant's body and often accomplished in a race or over a challenge course. The activity is approximately 15 years old. Its social world is miniscule compared with that of Association football (soccer), which is one of the world's oldest sports.

The composition of the social world was set out in the preceding chapter. The main point to be made in the present one is that belonging to and participating in the social world of a serious pursuit is, in general, a richly positive experience. Thus, it is most agreeable to talk shop with other participants, see how one's team is faring in the league's standings, discuss repairs of a prized musical instrument or item of sports equipment, search the Internet for information on the activity, and on and on. Audiences (fans, listeners, viewers, etc.) are normally an attractive part of this formation, although they can also be disappointing. The same holds for coaches, conductors, directors, teachers, mentors, and the like.

It is in their social world that participants estimate their own standing in the activity, achieved by comparing themselves with other members. That is, social worlds serve as the backdrop for gauging self-worth, for here is where the activity's standards of excellence are established, promulgated, and maintained. Excellence in the activity is embodied in exemplary individuals and, where pursued collectively, in exemplary teams. These are the stars of the activity's social world.

For all these reasons every social world is also an important wellspring of motivation, that being another facet of its positiveness. It can also be conceived of as a vast ensemble of resources for the participants, as in information, opportunities, services, supplies, network connections, among others.

Positive space

The word "space" in leisure studies is shorthand for three distinct angles from which to consider free-time activity. They are leisure space as institutional, temporal, and geographic. That is, leisure may be defined and examined for its fit in the social organization of the community and larger society; its place in the span of daily, weekly, and annual time;

DOI: 10.1057/9781137569943.0005

and its relationship to the surrounding physical environment (Cohen-Gewerc & Stebbins, 2013). The latter is often referred to as the geographic view of free-time activity.

Both geographic space and temporal space have special import for positive psychology. Leisure space understood in geographic terms has conventionally been referred to the places where leisure activities are pursued. These places may be natural, artificial, or a combination of both. Nowadays they may very well be virtual, as well (Crouch, 2006, p. 127). Natural, artificial, or virtual geographic space usually gives a distinctive positive flavor to the leisure activities in which individual participants are involved.

The conception of temporal space with most significance for positive psychology centers on the discretionary use of time, referred to in leisure studies as "discretionary time commitment" (Stebbins, 2006). This variety of commitment refers to the uncoerced, allocation of a certain number of minutes, hours, days, or other measure of time that a person devotes or would like to devote to carrying out a given activity. In other words, discretionary time commitment finds expression in leisure and in work where workers have some control over their time. In these areas of life the focus is always on particular activities and kinds of activities rather than on leisure in general.

Space and the serious pursuits

Sam Elkington (2014) explores how and in which ways space is experienced by participants when pursuing an amateur, hobbyist, or career volunteer activity. The SLP, he notes, has failed in the past to address the issue of space on the phenomenological level. In this respect we must note that space is not synonymous with place. Rather the first has an "aesthetic" meaning. Any given space "reveals a perceptual environment that joins a distinctive physical identity and coherence, a resonance, with a memorable character with which an individual actively engages through action" (Elkington, 2014, p. 96).

Serious leisure participants also develop a strong attachment to and identification with the space in which they pursue their core activities. Elkington states that the strength of this attachment is substantially determined by the capacity of that space to facilitate expressions of skill and knowledge and to generate desired experiences, among them, that

DOI: 10.1057/9781137569943.0005

of flow. He applies his ideas about the spatial meanings of serious leisure to all the core activities pursued there.

I have added in another article (Stebbins, 2013a) that Elkington's ideas also hold for devotee work and therefore for all the serious pursuits. Furthermore, it is possible to show how and where these meanings vary by category of core activity. We look next at a typology of the spatial meaning of the core activities around which the serious pursuits revolve (taken from Stebbins 2013a).

The spatial meaning of core activities

So far it has been possible to identify seven types of space for the serious pursuits. These seven types of spaces are perceivable through some or all of the following senses: visual, olfactory, tactile, and auditory (including little or no sound). Moreover, the core activities of some serious pursuits are spatially anchored in more than one of the seven types. Thus, athletes have a certain space to be conquered and another space for training, which they use as a resource. The painter has an atelier (resource) and one or more exhibition venues (showcase).

Conquered space

A wide variety of serious activities have as part of their core the conquering of some sort of space. That is, the special meaning of that space is constructed according to how it bears on the core activity being undertaken. Here we find the sports, board games, nature challenge activities, participation activities, and possibly others. For example, football players know at any time during a match that, if they are to win, so many yards or meters must be covered. In the "nature challenge activities" (Davidson & Stebbins, 2011), climbers for instance are aware of the height and other physical features of the mountain face they aim to ascend. Then there are the routes to be followed or spaces to be occupied in the various board games like chess, checkers, and cribbage.

As an example of the role of space in the participation activities, consider how it is conquered when fishing. First, there is the space in which fish are caught: open sea, trout stream, backwater bayou, local pond. Second, there is the question of the depth of water in, or on, which to fish: close to the bottom, just below the surface, on the surface (e.g., dry-fly fishing). The meaning of space is both complex and distinctive in such participant activities as caving, hunting, canoeing, and SCUBA diving.

Showcase space

Showcasing creative works is the realm of the fine arts and entertainment fields. The theater, concert hall, and comedy club exemplify one genre of space for displaying these efforts. Another is the variety of exhibition venues for presenting paintings, sculptures, and ceramic pieces, which include, depending on the art, shops, streets, offices, pedestrian corridors, and these days even some transportation terminals. Nonetheless, they do share some of their space with busking street performers, who may also present their acts in pedestrian corridors as well as along certain streets. Additionally, subway stations are a main space for some of these artists. Showcase space is different for writers. For them (and the liberal arts hobbyists who read their works), the book shop and the book fair are central and, increasingly, the Internet.

Resource space

This is space needed by amateurs, hobbyists, and occupational devotees to produce something or perform a service, a type that includes all the necessary equipment and supplies found within it. The scientist's laboratory is arguably the archetypical example. Although often less clearly defined, scientific field stations constitute another space for scientific core activity. Here observations of birds or insects are conducted or, looking upward, astronomical phenomena are viewed. Then there is the atelier for making and tinkering. Included here are the kitchen and woodworking shop as well as the miscellaneous locations in which the skilled trades operate, among them, the garage and the back garden (for gardening, work on old cars, etc.). In devotee work, construction sites and locations where repairs and maintenance are conducted (as in plumbing, heating, and roofing) exemplify resource space.

The study is the prized space for writers (when not showcasing their works). It is likewise for "committed readers," or those hobbyists who read extensively to acquire literary knowledge, a passion that necessarily takes time and requires concentration (Stebbins, 2013b). And paralleling this use of space for core activities are the places where musicians, dancers, athletes, and others go to maintain and perfect their skills.

DOI: 10.1057/9781137569943.0005

Sales space

For the occupational devotees in small business, the shop from which they vend their products or services is a special space. Along similar lines we find the public outlets for hobbyist makers of, say, quilts, knit goods, and ceramic objects. They sporadically – and for some even regularly – set up stands at craft fairs, shopping centers, and flea markets, among other places. Virtual space now enables an e-commerce in these businesses.

Helping space

This is the space from which help is provided. The help may be that of either volunteers or professionals, with the latter conceptualized as devotee workers. Among the second the offices of counselors and consultants serve as a main space within which they pursue their core activities. Other spaces for some of this group's core activities may include a home office, a public or institutional library, and a specialized book store. And these days counseling and consulting are sometimes provided over the Internet.

Career volunteers also have their distinctive spaces. These are evident to some extent by where they serve, as in a zoo or museum, on a board of directors (board room or equivalent), at a primary school, or at a hospital. This core activity space for volunteers who work to preserve or maintain the natural environment is a river, forest, or the town's park as well as the air we breathe, the water we drink, and the earth we inhabit. Recreational volunteers serve in spaces like camps, sport centers, municipal recreational facilities, and sites for sporting competitions (e.g., gymnasia, swimming pools, ski hills, running courses).

Virtual space

This is what Elkington has labeled "virtual space" (Elkington, S., personal communication, October 31, 2012). It is the home of, among other activities, the Internet-based serious pursuits. A main use of such space occurs during leisure-based surfing of the Web, the serious leisure expression of which is seen in the reading undertaken in pursuit of a liberal arts hobby. Another facet of this space is evident in skilled, knowledgeable gaming done in interaction in cyberspace with other people. In these examples and ones given in Sales space and Helping space, the space in question is our vague sense of what cyberspace actually is. It is impalpable,

DOI: 10.1057/9781137569943.0005

difficult to fathom, and, yet, real enough to leave its users with a unique spatial sense. Above all it is vast. So much so that John Perry Barlow, an American poet and essayist, once joked that "in Cyberspace, the 1st Amendment [in the American Constitution] is a local ordinance."

Tourist Space

Much of tourism is centered on space of some kind, including scenic vistas, architectural wonders, and urban streetscapes. For most tourists, seeing such attractions is a type of casual leisure, namely, sensory stimulation. More rarely, however, some tourists make a hobby of viewing and studying a particular type of space. Thus, conceivably, these enthusiasts might tour around the world to contemplate and be educated about, say, its tallest buildings, different old towns (where a city began), or ancient ruins. As an example Bauckham (2013) studied "groundhoppers" or people passionate about getting to know through direct observation the details of the many different (Association) football grounds on which the world game is routinely played.

To the extent that the serious pursuits deliver positive experiences for their participants, the space in which this occurs is also likely to be favorably evaluated and remembered. Yet, space can occasionally be problematic and therefore negative, which is another reason for intentionally considering it in leisure studies and positive psychology. In other words, what in the foregoing types of space might go wrong such that their usual positiveness is no longer present? A snowstorm on the (Canadian) football field? A computer breakdown while gaming in virtual space? An evening of excessive chatter and noise in a jazz club? In short, spatial positiveness is often a delicate condition, and by no means always within the participant's control.

The positive body

Some serious leisure participants also develop a strong attachment to and identification with the space in which they use their bodies to pursue their core activities. That is, body form or functioning, if not both, is seen as crucial and may become a condition of pride and fulfillment. Body builders, figure skaters, gymnasts, dancers (in a serious pursuit), and fashion models number among the amateur-professional and hobbyist groups motivated by this orientation.[1] True, all these activities

DOI: 10.1057/9781137569943.0005

would be difficult to perform optimally were the body of the performer even a little overweight. But that person's appealing shape also contributes substantially to the aesthetic execution of these activities, activities where excellence is also determined by form and beauty.

Neither space nor the body is common foci for theorists and researchers in positive psychology. Still, apropos the positive body, Perkins and Nakamura (2013, p. 148) have observed that a person's "main motivation for performing an athletic activity [can be] to experience the inherent pleasure, excitement, or expressiveness involved in moving the body during the activity itself." They are addressing themselves to the second facet of the positive body, namely, its well-functioning. Much of the time people have little or no sense of their bodies, that is, as long as they are healthy and in no pain. But in certain serious pursuits a body that works well or shows well during their execution is both an asset and a (fulfilling) reward in itself. Perkins and Nakamura understood this reward to be part of flow. The "runner's high" and "getting into one's stride" in a sport or other physical activity constitute evidence of this feeling.

Conclusions

Among the many points made about leisure and positiveness in this chapter is the one that a full picture of the first cannot be couched solely in terms of the second. Negativeness can and sometimes does raise its ugly head. The committed enthusiast perseveres nonetheless, staying with the activity through thick and thin while recognizing, too, that undesirable things will happen. Indeed, in the serious pursuits it is often a source of pride to be able to handle them with equanimity. Ironically, then, even negativeness in such leisure can, following subsequent reflection, sometimes end up being positive.

Note

1 Fashion modeling has never been examined using the SLP. Therefore let me theorize here that models in this activity display and thereby promote clothing and, in so doing, may be understood as engaging in a kind of amateur or professional commercial theater. That is, they present their apparel ("costume") on a runway ("stage"), according to a script (walking along the runway while enacting prescribed bodily movements), and then acting it

DOI: 10.1057/9781137569943.0005

out by actually making these bodily movements. Moreover, some sort of *maquillage* is required. There is no speaking part here, which however, is not essential in theater (c.f., miming, various walk-on roles).

References

Bandura, A. (1997). *Self-efficacy: The exercise of control.* New York: Freeman.

Bauckham, D. (2013). Serious leisure: The case of groundhopping. In T. Blackshaw (Ed.), *Routledge handbook of leisure studies* (pp. 443–455). London: Routledge.

Cohen-Gewerc, E., & Stebbins, R.A. (2013). *Serious leisure and individuality.* Montreal, QC & Kingston, ON: McGill-Queens University Press.

Crouch, D. (2006). Geographies of leisure. In C. Rojek, S.M. Shaw, & A.J. Veal (Eds.), *A handbook of leisure studies* (pp. 125–139). Houndmills, Basingstoke, UK: Palgrave Macmillan.

Csikszentmihalyi, M. (1990). *Flow: The psychology of optimal experience.* New York: Harper & Row.

Dattilo, J., & Murphy, W.D. (1991). *Leisure education program planning: A systematic approach.* State College, PA: Venture.

Davidson, L., & Stebbins, R.A. (2011). *Serious leisure and nature: Sustainable consumption in the outdoors.* Houndmills, UK: Palgrave Macmillan.

Elkington, S. (2014). Sites of serious leisure. In S. Elkington & S. Gammon (Eds.), *Leisure in mind: Meaning, motives, and learning* (pp. 93–111). London: Routledge.

Lambdin, L. (1997). *Elderlearning.* Phoenix, AZ: Oryx Press.

Leitner, M.J., & Leitner, S.F. (2004). *Leisure enhancement*, 3rd ed. New York: Haworth.

Perkins, K., & Nakamura, J. (2013). Flow and leisure. In Freire, T. (Ed.), *Positive leisure science: From subjective experience to social contexts* (pp. 141–158). Dordrecht, the Netherlands: Springer.

Roberson, D.N., Jr. (2005). Leisure and learning: An investigation of older adults and self-directed learning. *Leisure/Loisir*, 29, 203–238.

Seligman, M.E.P., & Csikszentmihalyi, M. (2000). Positive psychology: An introduction. *American Psychologist*, 55(1), 5–14.

Selman, G., Cooke, M., Selman, M., & Dampier, P. (1998). *The foundations of adult education in Canada*, 2nd ed. Toronto, ON: Thompson Educational Publishing.

DOI: 10.1057/9781137569943.0005

Stebbins, R.A. (2004/2014). *Between work and leisure: The common ground of two separate worlds*. New Brunswick, NJ: Transaction Publishers. (paperback edition with new Preface, 2014).

Stebbins, R.A. (2005). *Challenging mountain nature: Risk, motive, and lifestyle in three hobbyist sports*. Calgary, AB: Detselig.

Stebbins, R.A. (2006). Discretionary time commitment: Effects on leisure choice and lifestyle. *Leisure Studies Association Newsletter*, 74 (July), 18–20. (also available at www.seriousleisure.net – Digital Library, "Leisure Reflections No. 12").

Stebbins, R.A. (2009). *Personal decisions in the public square: Beyond problem solving into a positive sociology*. New Brunswick, NJ: Transaction.

Stebbins, R.A. (2013a). The spaces of the serious pursuits: A typology. *Leisure Studies Association Newsletter*, 95 (July), 21–24 (also available at www.seriousleisure.net/Digital Library, "Leisure Reflections No. 33").

Stebbins, R.A. (2013b). *The committed reader: Reading for utility, pleasure and fulfillment in the twenty-first century*. Lanham, MD: Scarecrow.

DOI: 10.1057/9781137569943.0005

3
Interpersonal Relationships

Abstract: *Covered here are the main positive emotions found in four interpersonal relationships that are also commonly maintained through leisure activities. These emotions are acceptance, love (passionate/companionate), sympathy, and admiration/respect. They are aroused in the following relationships: spousal/partner, friendship, teacher–student, and mentoring. A definition of fundamental emotions is presented. Mentors, conceived of as altruistic volunteers, are distinguished from coaches, advisors, personal trainers, and private teachers and tutors. Interpersonal relationships are not themselves leisure activities, but rather arrangements in life within which leisure can be pursued in its three forms. Put otherwise, leisure – activity engaged in as human behavior (mental, physical, or both) – can give concrete expression to positive interpersonal relationships.*

Keywords: acceptance; admiration; friendships; interpersonal relationship; love; mentoring; respect; spousal/partner relationships; sympathy; teacher–student relationships

Stebbins, Robert A. *Leisure and Positive Psychology: Linking Activities with Positiveness.* Basingstoke: Palgrave Macmillan, 2015. DOI: 10.1057/9781137569943.0006.

This chapter opens with a discussion of the main positive emotions found in four interpersonal relationships that are also commonly maintained through leisure activities. The emotions are acceptance, love, sympathy, and admiration/respect. They are aroused in the following relationships: spousal/partner, friendship, teacher–student, and mentoring. Of course, other positive emotions also find occasional expression in these relationships, but the four just mentioned appear to be the most prevalent and the most crucial to dyadic strength.

Note, however, that on occasion negative interpersonal relationships also plague our lives. They are mostly ignored in this chapter, though it should be recognized that agreeable ties can sour: the married couple breaks up, the boss–employee relationship gets bitter, or two neighbors start feuding. These unhappy ties are further evidence for the observation that the positive features of life can never be taken for granted – instead they usually require careful nurturing.

The main part of the chapter is devoted to examining how casual, serious, and project-based leisure (all discussed in Chapter 1) work to bring positiveness to the four relationships just mentioned. Moreover, some interpersonal relationships endure for many years, having thus their own distinctive, positive histories.

Spousal/partner relationships

Since this is our first substantial encounter in this book with the concept of emotion, it is good to be as clear as possible from the outset on its meaning. To this end, Robinson's (2009) three criteria for defining fundamental emotions bring some needed clarity. He states that emotions:

1 have a strongly motivating subjective quality, like pleasure or pain;
2 are in response to a real or imagined event or object;
3 motivate specific types of behaviour or actions.

In line with the American Psychological Association's definition, I wish to add with reference to number 1 that an emotion is a complex pattern of changes involving physiological arousal, feelings, and cognitive processes and that, with reference to number 2, the real or imagined event is perceived as personally significant (http://www.apa.org/research/action/glossary.aspx).

DOI: 10.1057/9781137569943.0006

The emotions covered in this book have been identified as such by one or more of the following: Robinson (2009), Parrott (2001), and Plutchik (2001). This is not to argue that their lists are the last word on this difficult-to-define idea, but only that they have the scholarly authority to make plausible assertions in this area.

Spouses and partners can conceivably share in any of the three forms of leisure. Thus, in the serious pursuits, they might golf, hunt, or practice law together. They might go together on a sightseeing tour or take in a fireworks display (casual leisure). Possibly less often they might participate together on a leisure project, as in volunteering for a local arts festival or in landscaping the property around their home.

What is the positive emotional content generated by mutual participation in these activities? For one, acceptance (Plutchik, 2001) is felt in the behavior associated with these various leisure activities. For example, a couple playing violin duets might observe how well they just played them or how much they had improved since their previous attempt. This emotion would also be aroused when one of them suggests that they set aside some time for playing the duets, and when, say several days after the last musical session, one of them observes how rewarding that session was (possibly during a session of casual conversation).

Yet, leisure acceptance in interpersonal relationships can extend beyond mutual participation to the arrangement wherein the partner willingly allows the other to engage in leisure that the first does not do. But this extension, evidence suggests, is far from universal. In the serious pursuits of quilting and barbershop singing, for example (Stalp, 2007, p. 130; Stebbins, 1996, pp. 77–80), some spouses were found only to tolerate their partner's activity and a smaller number even to oppose it.

Turning to love Hatfield (1988) distinguishes between the passionate and companionate varieties. The first identifies the intense sexual arousal and affection sometimes felt in a romantic union, whereas the second refers, rather more nebulously, to the more or less steady close bonding of two people over many years as their lives intersect in myriad ways. In some spousal/partner relationships the two may be both lovers and companions. In Plutchik's "circumplex model" love and acceptance are neighboring emotions among the several radial dimensions.

Unless speaking of passionate love as expressed in sexual activities (a kind of sensual casual leisure), all three forms of leisure admit expressions of love, though it appears, mainly of the companionate variety. In this emotional scenario acceptance is joined with a sense of being together with a loved

DOI: 10.1057/9781137569943.0006

person while engaged in a mutually attractive activity. Does companionate love become richer when experienced in the satisfaction of casual leisure (excluding having sex) vis-à-vis the fulfillment found in project-based leisure and the serious pursuits? And, conversely, is the satisfaction or fulfillment enriched by companionship? We do not know the answers yet, although the two questions are certainly amenable to empirical study.

Then there is the emotion of sympathy, which is by no means found only in the domain of leisure. That is, we might sympathize with a partner or spouse who has problems at work or faces an unpleasant nonwork obligation like caring for a sick relative or undergoing a root canal procedure at the hands of the dentist. In leisure, the only domain that is predominantly positive, is there ever need for sympathy?

Yes, albeit sporadically and then largely in the serious pursuits. A man might sympathize with his partner and gourmet cook one of whose confections for the evening dinner party is not turning out as well as hoped. A woman who has trained assiduously for a marathon run only to sprain her ankle while on the course might (dare we say "should") find some comforting sympathy from her husband.

Finally, let us consider the place of admiration/respect in the leisure zone of interpersonal relationships. As with some of the other positive emotions covered in this section, admiration/respect is most likely to be felt during serious activities and during some of the projects. Here there is something of substance to admire (e.g., achievement, perseverance, effort). The leisure in question might be mutual, as in the couple who golf together or volunteer at the same senior's center while respecting the other's ability at the activity. Or respect could be one-sided. For instance, a man admires his wife's poetry; a woman admires her husband's wood carvings.

Admiration and respect, as with sympathy, are not limited to the domain of leisure activities. Thus, we can admire our partner's ability to remain at a paying job under difficult conditions (e.g., crabby boss, excessive noise, heavy lifting). Nonwork obligations can engender respect, as in persevering at the (personally defined) unpleasant task of keeping the family car in decent running order.

Friendships

In most instances two friends seem to accept each other's leisure activities, even if they share only some of them. This is because friendships

DOI: 10.1057/9781137569943.0006

are typically much more segmented than marriages and partnerships. In other words, the former tend to be founded on particular roles and activities, and may never expand beyond one or two of them. So, some people have work friends with whom after hours in a bar or restaurant they occasionally enjoy some sociable conversation. Those same people might well have other friends, where the bond revolves around a shared passion for, say, kayaking, playing poker, or volunteering for a political party. Acceptance of friends is generally related to the few activities they do together. By contrast marriages and partnerships are far more encompassing, for the pair usually know all the other's interests, possibly participating in some of them and often accepting the rest.

Following Hatfield's definition, love in friendships can only be of the companionate variety. One exception to this generalization is the chummy practice known these days as "hooking up," or arranging for a passionate sexual relationship that lasts one or a few sessions. Nevertheless, as friendships go, hooking up would number among the shortest instances of this type of interpersonal relationship.

Sympathy and admiration/respect in the realm of friendship seem to follow the same patterns observed in spousal/partnership relationships. The principle difference is probably centered on the narrowness of the first compared with the breadth of the second. Quite simply, the segmented nature of the typical friendship admits of fewer opportunities for expressing these emotions.

Teacher/student relationships

These relationships form at their deepest in primary and secondary education and in technical and university education beyond the level of mass instruction. I will confine discussion here to those of substantial depth, where the pair comes to know each other in sufficient detail to facilitate the principal educational goals of the relationship. It would be stretching the definition of interpersonal relationship to maintain that such exists between a student and a professor when the latter is teaching a large class of, say, more than 300 enrolees. In any case a tie under these conditions is normally comparatively superficial.

Wherein lies the leisure component of this relationship as manifested in its deepest senses? It is absent in the primary and secondary educational relationships, mainly because these students have no choice but to

DOI: 10.1057/9781137569943.0006

attend school. This is coerced activity, whereas leisure is not. This is not to ignore that they sometimes like their school involvements, but only to underscore the criterion that, in true leisure, participants may abandon what the activities being pursued.

It is different beyond high school in the area of higher education (Stebbins, 2014, chapter 3). Here in universities and four-year colleges pre-professional student-amateurs take courses sequenced into larger specialized formal programs, engage in practical work, and thereby learn just how fulfilling their future profession can be. In this milieu they develop a substantial devotion to their future profession. The practical work gives them the opportunity to do at least some of the core tasks done by their professional counterparts. All this occurs in an atmosphere that is essentially one of serious leisure, in that students can and do at times quit these training programs, giving substance to their basically uncoercive nature. Evidence from a British study supports the proposition that they love what they do.

> Many students say they are pursuing their subject out of love, and that education is an end in itself. Some give little thought to where the qualification might lead. In one study of British PhD graduates, about a third admitted that they were doing their doctorate partly to go on being a student, or put off job hunting. Nearly half of engineering students admitted to this. (*The Economist*, 2010)

But are there not students in these programs who feel obligated to be there, as by parental pressure or a desire to make money however disagreeable the training required to reach this goal? Probably so. For them being a student seems best described as a lengthy nonwork obligation.

All this pertains to the professions serving patients and clients. The analogous situation for amateurs learning the public-centered professions is much fuzzier. Stebbins (2014, chapter 3) shows that informal and adult-education-style learning suffices for many of the four types of amateurs. Nevertheless, in art and science, participants may acquire college or university diplomas in their passion, the majority of them hoping to find work in it, to become public-centered professionals. True, the diploma is a kind of certification. But it is also true that uncertified amateurs are also pursuing – sometimes quite successfully – the same artistic or scientific activity. In other words, the public-centered pros lack the substantial degree of control over who enters their callings that the client-centered pros enjoy (Stebbins, 1992, pp. 28–30). The same may

DOI: 10.1057/9781137569943.0006

be said for students in formal training programs leading to certification in a trade (Stebbins, 2014, chapter 7).

The emotions

Acceptance can be crucial in the teacher–student relationships that develop in education at the postsecondary level. Obviously for positive bonds the student must accept, at minimum, the teacher's ways of teaching and the content being taught. And for the relationship to flourish, the teacher must accept the student's ways of learning, level of enthusiasm for this process, and capacity for learning what the teacher presents. Compatible personalities are also likely to be important considerations in acceptance.

The student–teacher relationship is built mostly if not entirely on learning how to enact a serious pursuit. The main reward for the student is self-fulfillment, the most common components of which are a combination of self-actualization, self-enrichment, and self-expression (Stebbins, 2007/2015, pp. 13–14). This is, perhaps, more obvious for the amateur/student than for the professional/teacher. Still, the latter is also striving for fulfillment, albeit in the devotee work role of teaching and guiding. Acceptance in both individuals suggests that the relationship is fostering fulfillment for each, even though the fulfillment is differently experienced, in part because it has different content.

Acceptance in the teacher–student relationship revolves around intellectual matters: gaining and imparting knowledge, information, and understanding. It may also include occupational guidance and facilitation by the teacher for the student. Finally, imparting knowledge, information, and understanding is sometimes a two-way process, exemplified in students who collaborate with a professor as authors of articles, critical readers of manuscripts, research assistants, and the like.

In most instances, it appears, such acceptance spawns growth of a friendship between the two, which endures at least until the student graduates from the program. Some last much longer, however, as when certain of the above-mentioned collaborations continue or the student lands a position in the teacher's department. In harmony with the earlier discussion of friendships, the teacher/student relationship is also typically segmented.

Admiration does not necessarily follow from acceptance. In other words, a teacher or student might accept the scholarly or pedagogical

DOI: 10.1057/9781137569943.0006

ways of the other without admiring them. For admiration, in particular, has to do with wonder, esteem, and reverence of the other's performance in a serious pursuit in which both share an intense interest. Respect, on the other hand, does appear to be a necessary condition for acceptance. How could either a teacher or a student accept the other's involvements in the shared activity without also respecting that person? Rolley's (2012) review of the relevant literature, along with her own study in australia, confirms that respect for teachers from students and the wider community is essential for their well-being. The same was true for the students as respected by their teachers.

Thomas Mann, a twentieth-century author and social critic, once observed that: "I have always been an admirer. I regard the gift of admiration as indispensable if one is to amount to something; I don't know where I would be without it." Inspiration through "memorable contact" with admirable figures has always been an important contingency early in many of the careers in the serious pursuits (Stebbins, 2014, chapter 2). Any number of students would make the same observation about certain teachers.

The emotion of sympathy, when called for, fits nicely in all this. Where there is acceptance and especially admiration and respect in the teacher/student relationship, we should expect sympathy from the second when the first is, say, seriously ill, injured in an accident, or forced out of teaching by a mandatory retirement policy. Such illness or injury on the part of the student might well spark sympathy in that person's professor.

Mentoring

Elsewhere I have written about mentoring as a leisure activity, in particular a kind of volunteering (Stebbins, 2006). A mentor is someone who, with regard to a specified area of life, is both trusted and respected by a protégé, or mentee, where trust and respect are based on a significant level of experience and knowledge that the latter believes the former to have. Superiority in this regard is critical, for why would the mentee accept an equal, or an inferior, in this role when superior experience and knowledge are what this person seeks. Some mentoring programs are formal; they are organized by and carried out within a formal organization. The many programs for youth and immigrants, for example, train mentors to work with such people within an organizational context.

DOI: 10.1057/9781137569943.0006

Yet, a good deal of mentoring, indeed possibly most of it, takes place elsewhere, on an informal plane.

The roles of private teacher and private tutor resemble that of a mentor. But, to the extent the first two get remunerated for their efforts, as a partial or full-time livelihood (which seems to happen often), they begin to separate themselves from the third. Additionally teachers and tutors are commonly paid to perform a widely recognized, albeit specialized, service such as giving piano lessons or instructing in a language. Here the deeper personal involvement typical of the mentor–mentee relationship is normally absent. That is, consonant with what was said earlier the student–teacher, student–tutor tie is less intimate, enduring, and broad-ranging compared with the one a mentor has with a mentee. But when a teacher or tutor provides the desired service free of charge, as the leisured mentor does exclusively, all three roles begin to blur. By the way the mentor–mentee relationship, though profound, is nonetheless still typically one that is segmented. In other words this dyad is not as broad-ranging as, say, the marital dyad or even a long and deep friendship, two kinds of ties that commonly encompass many areas of each person's life.

Furthermore, at least in Western society, teachers, tutors, and mentors have come to be differentiated from "coaches." Today the latter constitute an occupational role, in the sense that they count on it as a livelihood. And, according to the website of the International Coach Federation (www.coachfederation.org), coaches are in the process of professionalizing.

Yet all four advising roles, mentoring included, share the same hoped-for outcome: improved attainment of important goals and enhanced personal lifestyle of a protégé, or in the case of the coach, a client, both accomplished through a one-on-one relationship with an advisor. As for personal trainers they, too, can be seen as part of the coaching group, in that this expert offers a remunerated, specialized service centered, in this instance, on the diet, habits, lifestyle, and physical conditioning of, typically, wealthy clients. Moreover some coaches serve not only individuals, but also various groups. They may advertise their expertise in working with teams.

For the unpaid teacher, tutor, and mentor, their services are, at bottom, a kind of leisure. This assertion rests on the assumption that unpaid mentoring (teaching, tutoring) is also uncoerced activity, pursued because the mentor (teacher, tutor, advisor) finds it in some

DOI: 10.1057/9781137569943.0006

way agreeable.[1] More particularly, mentoring results in a distinctive kind of career, one that unfolds as serious leisure volunteering. In other words, mentoring is distinct from tutoring, coaching, and the like, in part, because the former lasts significantly longer both as a role and as a foundation for a deepening interpersonal relationship. As in all volunteering – this holds as well for tutoring, teaching, and coaching – there also is a target of benefits, namely the protégé. Yet, only mentoring is substantially motivated by a focused altruism, a strongly held attitude (and accompanying emotion) that disposes the mentor to help another out of concern for that person's welfare or satisfaction, if not both. Nevertheless, though altruism is a quintessential feature of volunteering, research makes clear that, generally, volunteering is also motivated by a self-serving, self-interested component (Musick & Wilson, 2008, chapter 4).

Becoming a mentor

It is possible that many mentors, especially those taking up the role for the first time, have only a sketchy idea of the rewards awaiting them. If abruptly asked to serve as mentor by a would-be mentee, the flattery or honor of being thus invited by this person may be sufficient to encourage the first to accept the invitation. Of course there will be details to negotiate, for example what the mentor must do, when, where, how, and how often. And the needs of the second may be such that the first feels unable to meet them, the result being that the anticipated mentoring relationship fails to take off.

Other mentoring relationships would seem to drift into place, with neither party being fully aware until long into the relationship that this has happened. Indeed, there are probably objectively classifiable mentoring relationships that neither person recognizes as such. So, a friend or relative might serve for years in this capacity in a certain area of life, with little or no sense that this dyad is significantly based on mentoring. Mentoring can therefore occur unknowingly, accomplishing what mentors and mentees everywhere generally hope to gain, namely, reaching the important goals and enhancing the personal lifestyle of the latter. The mentor may be linguistically a mentor, as defined in ancient Greece, but this role in modern Western society is far from being universally recognized by that title.

DOI: 10.1057/9781137569943.0006

Emotions in mentoring

The patterns of emotional expressions in mentoring follow closely those of the teacher–student relationship. Acceptance is axiomatic in both, for without it neither could exist. Since mentorship usually rests on the mentor's deep understanding of the mentee, companionate love is probably to be expected. Passionate love in these two relationships, though not mentioned until this point in this chapter, is also possible, even while being morally questionable. Such love is clearly positive emotion, but nevertheless it could undermine the authority and expertise the teacher and mentor have to give to the goals of the student and the mentee.

Deterioration of the relationship seems especially probable when the love is exploitative; when one of the pair uses the bond to exact sexual favors. Here love is a positive emotion only for the person doing the exploiting. In such circumstances, admiration and respect – normally a feature in mentorship as well – are likely to be shaken, particularly for the party who has been exploited.

As in the teacher–student relationship the mentor or mentee may occasionally feel sympathy for the other and probably for the same reasons. Again, because mentorship is usually more encompassing of each person's life, the scope for sympathy is correspondingly broadened. For example, a mentor might receive sympathy from a mentee sparked by the death of the mentor's family pet or the failure to win a coveted award in a hobbyist competition, events that might not be shared with a student, for example.

Conclusions

It should be understood that interpersonal relationships are not themselves leisure, but rather arrangements in life within which leisure can be pursued in its three forms. Put otherwise, leisure – activity engaged in as human behavior (mental, physical, or both) – can give concrete expression to positive interpersonal relationships like the ones covered in this chapter. Moreover, it can provide avenues for positive emotional expression that can enhance bonding and strengthen further the ties between the two parties. The adage "a family that plays together stays together" recognizes this contribution to our well-being that we are able to make in free time.

DOI: 10.1057/9781137569943.0006

Interpersonal relationships are pervasive. As evidence of this, they and the leisure activities pursued within them, bear on every chapter in this book. Moreover, these relationships and their activities can be incubators both of self-fulfillment and a valued identity in a serious pursuit. How this works in real terms is shown in, among the other chapters to be covered, the next one on contemplation and spirituality.

Note

1 To the extent that remunerated coaches meet the criteria for devotee workers, they too are engaged in a serious pursuit.

References

The Economist (2010). Doctoral degrees: The disposable academic, December 16, Online edition.

Hatfield, E. (1988). Passionate and companionate love. In R.J. Sternberg & M.L. Barnes (Eds.), *The psychology of love* (pp. 191–217). New Haven, CT: Yale University Press.

Musick, M.A., & Wilson, J. (2008). *Volunteers: A social profile.* Bloomington, IN: Indiana University Press.

Parrott, W.G. (Ed.) (2001). *Emotions in social psychology: Key readings.* New York: Psychology Press.

Plutchik, R. (2001). The nature of emotions: Human emotions have deep evolutionary roots, a fact that may explain their complexity and provide tools for clinical practice. *American Scientist*, 89(4), 344–350.

Robinson, D.L. (2009). Brain function, mental experience and personality. *The Netherlands Journal of Psychology*, 64, 152–167.

Rolley, S (2012). Pupil wellbeing – teacher wellbeing: Two sides of the same coin? *Educational & Child Psychology*, 29(4), 8–17.

Stalp, M. B. (2007). *Quilting: The fabric of everyday life.* New York: Berg.

Stebbins, R.A. (1992). *Amateurs, professionals, and serious leisure.* Montreal, QC and Kingston, ON: McGill-Queen's University Press.

Stebbins, R.A. (1996). *The barbershop singer: Inside the social world of a musical hobby.* Toronto, ON: University of Toronto Press.

DOI: 10.1057/9781137569943.0006

Stebbins, R.A. (2006). Mentoring as a leisure activity: On the informal world of small-scale altruism. *World Leisure Journal*, 48(4), 3–10.

Stebbins, R.A. (2007/2015). *Serious leisure: A perspective for our time*. New Brunswick, NJ/: Transaction. (paperback edition with new Preface, 2015).

Stebbins, R.A. (2014). *From dabbling to devotee work: Careers in long-term self-fulfillment*. Houndmills, UK: Palgrave Macmillan.

DOI: 10.1057/9781137569943.0006

4
Contemplation and Spirituality

Abstract: *Two emotions are considered in this chapter, namely, awe and enthrallment, they being the two prominent emotional outcomes of contemplation and spirituality. For the purposes of this chapter, contemplation and reflection are treated of as synonyms; both terms refer to the act of thinking about something. Such thinking, or concentration, may be highly focused or more general as in getting into a certain mood. Informal observations suggest that contemplation comes in at least four types. Three of these types refer to serious reflection, with the fourth type referring to a kind of casual leisure. Spirituality is, at least initially, a mental state, specifically one of profound regard for the spiritual, for the nonmaterial. Subsequently, however, the search for spirituality may evolve into a way of life. Heintzman argues that spiritual wellness may be thought of as a benefit of leisure.*

Keywords: awe; casual leisure; contemplation; enthrallment; flow; serious leisure; spirituality

Stebbins, Robert A. *Leisure and Positive Psychology: Linking Activities with Positiveness*. Basingstoke: Palgrave Macmillan, 2015. DOI: 10.1057/9781137569943.0007.

 DOI: 10.1057/9781137569943.0007

The two relevant emotions considered in this chapter are awe and enthrallment, they being two prominent outcomes of contemplation and spirituality. Awe and enthrallment will first be defined in some detail, thereby enabling us to place both within the SLP. These emotions will then be considered as they are aroused by contemplation, spirituality, and the leisure that is found in both.

Awe and enthrallment

Keltner and Haidt (2003) hold that awe relates to pleasure, but may also accompany fear. We can be in awe of events (e.g., waterfalls or scenes of devastation) or objects (e.g., a work of art or a fearful animal). It consists of a perception of vastness and a need for accommodation in that the individual is unable to assimilate the awe-inspiring event or object into his or her current mental structures. Awe is thus aroused by threat, beauty, virtue, exceptional ability, and the supernatural.

We can be in awe of most anything perceivable with the senses. To understand in detail how awe and leisure activities go together, let us look at the way Davidson and Stebbins (2011, pp. 6–7) incorporated this emotion into their study of nature challenge activities (hobbies and amateur pursuits centered on meeting a natural test posed by air, water, land, flora, fauna, or ice and snow). Their study explored systematically the proposition that a nature challenge activity (NCA) is pursued in the awe-inspiring natural environment of that activity. For mountain kayakers, for instance, their wonder-filled environment had, among other features, the sound, sight, and feel of the rushing mountain rivers and creeks and the rock, earth, trees, and vegetation through which they flow. Snowboarders were in awe of the snow-filled back-country setting through which they rode as it descended, often precipitously, before them. The mountain climbers loved rock, its nooks, crannies, and solidity (when present) and the way these qualities and others combined to create a sense of being suspended in air far above the base of the steep slopes they mounted. Borrie and Roggenbuck (2001) reviewed a number of studies that have measured emotion, mood, attention states, and feelings of connection with nature. The two authors learned from their research that intense awe of the environment can be variable, depending on what participants are doing, how long they have been doing it, meteorological conditions, and the like.

DOI: 10.1057/9781137569943.0007

Davidson and Stebbins pondered several alternatives to awe and wonderment. Two of these were "euphoria" and "exhilaration," which though rejected, they nevertheless regarded as closely synonymous with awe. Another was "spirituality," refused because of its oftentimes close association with religion. Some people in an NCA might well describe the experience precisely this way, but others would not. "Delight" would have served their purposes were it not for its sense of pleasure. Casual leisure generates pleasure, whereas the central rewards of the serious pursuits are deeper. In brief, the authors were trying to communicate with both noun and adjective (awe-inspiring, wonder-filled) the "wow" feeling – the positive emotion – of an aesthetic encounter with nature, as experienced during normal conduct of the pursuit's core activity.

Enthrallment, by contrast, is the state of being mentally or morally captivated by some pleasing object or thought. Parrott (2001) lists enthrallment as a secondary emotion and again as a tertiary emotion, this time alongside rapture. The primary emotion is joy, suggesting that enthrallment is wholly positive, whereas awe can be either positive or negative. We may also say that the perceived events or objects arousing awe are not necessarily, perhaps not even usually, enthralling or captivating. Perhaps this is because enthrallment is primarily focused on ideas and the capacity of certain ones to engulf those who ponder them. In enthrallment one is literally lost in thought about the nature and meaning of an object, event, or idea.

Contemplation

For the purposes of this chapter, contemplation and reflection are treated of as synonyms; both terms refer to the act of thinking about something. Such thinking, or concentration, may be highly focused or more general as in getting into a certain mood. When contemplating (reflecting) we make thought on a particular subject the center of our attention, the dominant activity of the moment. As an activity that endures over time, running in length from a few seconds to possibly an hour or more, it is however largely mental, even though the contemplator might manipulate related objects during this period. Contemplation may be intense and relatively impermeable – which if positive is essentially enthrallment – or it may be relatively permeable, where a person's thoughts are easily interrupted by environmental stimuli.

DOI: 10.1057/9781137569943.0007

My informal observations suggest that contemplation comes in at least four types (Stebbins, 2006). One is *obligatory contemplation*, a process forced on us from time to time, as we try in certain areas of life to solve problems from which we cannot escape. This type commonly occurs in conjunction with either a work or a nonwork obligation, and on these two occasions, the problems reflected on are legion: how to approach the boss for a raise, smooth over soured relations with a spouse, most effectively fill in the annual tax return, to mention a few.

Two, *casual leisure contemplation* is, by contrast, not coerced, but is rather taken up as a form of casual leisure of the play variety. This is reflection, or speculation, for the fun of it, as exemplified in the lyrics of the song "If I were a Rich Man" from the Broadway show *Fiddler on the Roof*. How many of us have speculated about what we might do with the money gained from winning the lottery? Playing with ideas, as sometimes happens even in intellectual circles, is another instance of casual leisure contemplation.

Three, there is also *serious leisure as contemplation*, or reflection devoted to solving a problem arising with regard to a serious leisure activity. Although this is not play, it is nevertheless uncoerced, in that the activity itself is uncoerced. This kind of reflection occurs when, for example, a participant considers the best training approach for an upcoming marathon, ponders which of two musical instruments to buy, or reflects on the pros and cons of a prospective volunteer role.

Four, *contemplation as serious leisure* is the classificatory home of complex reflective activity engaged in for its own sake. The activity is complex, for if a participant is to learn how to execute it, this person must acquire special skills and a body of knowledge to go with them. This type – sometimes called "meditation" – is exemplified by such systems as Yoga, Tai Chi, and transcendental meditation. Meditation, or contemplation, in search of spirituality as guided by the Christian religion is a further example (Doohan, 1990, among others, examines the link between leisure and spirituality). Some forms of specifically religious meditation, to be effective, require, in addition to knowledge of technique, knowledge of the religious system from which the first receives its inspiration.

Contemplation as serious leisure would seem to be most accurately classified as a hobby of the activity participant variety. Activity participation is the classificatory home of noncompetitive, rule-based, pursuits, and there are certainly many rules and procedures incorporated in the

DOI: 10.1057/9781137569943.0007

meditative systems mentioned in the preceding paragraph. Further, in every such system, rules abound on how to behave with reference to other people and objects in the settings in which meditation occurs. Serious leisure contemplation is similar to what Tanquerey (1924) called "acquired contemplation," in contradistinction to "infused contemplation," or that instilled in a person by God.

The social and physical places in which contemplation occurs are many and varied. Thus, we are capable of reflecting, to some extent, in a crowded, noisy room, providing that we can nevertheless remain focused on our line of thought. It is likely, however, that most contemplation in such places is of the casual type. Otherwise, most serious reflection (types 1, 3, and 4) seems most effectively carried out while alone, as in one's own study or bedroom, out in nature, or at an institutional retreat.[1] I have argued that one of the main benefits of aloneness, or solitude, is to put the individual in this optimal social state where intense, uninterrupted thought can occur (Stebbins, 1993, chap. 9). And it follows from what has been said so far that repairing to one's room, to nature, or to an institutionalized retreat for contemplative reasons is not necessarily a leisure activity (see Ouellette & Carette, 2004). When not leisure, the retreater may have been coerced into trying to solve, through reflection, a nagging, unpleasant problem. However obligatory and unpleasant the problem to be solved (if that is why solitude is sought), monastic retreats can still be pleasant places, given the quiet found there, the beauty of the architecture, chanting of the monks, agreeableness of the natural setting, and for some, being closer to God.

Spirituality

How does contemplation relate to spirituality? Whatever else it might be, spirituality is, at least initially, a mental state, specifically one of profound regard for the spiritual, for the nonmaterial. Subsequently, however, the search for spirituality may evolve into a way of life. This is one sense of the concept. Spirituality in these two senses is also an important product, or outcome, of some, though not all, contemplation. It appears to be, most clearly, a product of certain sessions of casual leisure contemplation as well as all sessions of serious leisure as contemplation, whereas the other two types are too problem-oriented to be qualified as spiritual. Thus, we might casually think about the vastness, beauty, or purpose of

DOI: 10.1057/9781137569943.0007

breathtaking scenery, finding in the process, a kind of spirituality. And the spirituality reached though serious leisure meditation, for example, is part of the intended result of such activity.

Contemplation as leisure

Today, in leisure studies, contemplation as a distinct, free-time activity seems to have become largely forgotten. Yet, in the philosophic backdrop to the field, contemplation had been an important player. Aristotle (1915) is widely recognized for his observation that finding time for leisurely contemplation is a main goal of work; that the reason for working is to sustain life, thus giving us an opportunity to contemplate. Much more recently Pieper (1963), a Catholic philosopher who followed Aristotle's line of reasoning, viewed contemplation as a special form of leisure, during which the individual is enabled to think about and communicate with God. And all leisure was undertaken for intrinsic reasons. About the same time de Grazia (1962, p. 18) held that "the man in contemplation is a free man. He needs nothing. Therefore nothing determines or distorts his thought. He does whatever he loves to do, and what he does is done for its own sake." Psychologist John Neulinger (1974, p. 5) observed that, gradually in philosophic thought, the ideal of contemplation gave way to a search for understanding using nature's laws, at first through astrology, but later by way of medicine.

This change in intellectual orientation seems still with us in that the idea of contemplation is not often discussed. Still, a few exceptions exist, among them the ideas of Doohan mentioned earlier. Moreover Paddick (1982) lamented the paltry amount of time that modern humankind commonly sets aside for "contemplation of ends." He blamed "education for leisure" for this sad situation, since such education tends to stress popular activities, of which contemplation is certainly no example. Ouellette and Carette (2004) studied a sample of 521 men who spent up to seven days in contemplation, among other activities, during a personal retreat at a Canadian monastery, the Abbaye Saint-Benoît, in Québec (see also Ouellette, Kaplan, & Kaplan, 2005). Their findings show that, for most of those who answered the questionnaire, the contemplation engaged in at the monastery (the authors used the term "reflection") may be classified, using the scheme developed in the present article, as obligatory. As such it is uncertain whether it is leisure.

DOI: 10.1057/9781137569943.0007

Nonetheless, the pressing need to reflect on a difficult problem sometimes emerged in the pleasant monastic environment only after the retreater had developed a relaxed frame of mind. Here leisure may be transformed into an activity driven by a felt obligation to try to solve a problem. Interest in the Ouellete and Carette paper, and another issuing from the same project (Ouellette, Heintzman, & Carette, 2005), centers primarily on "psychological restoration," a central concept in Attention Restoration Theory (e.g., Kaplan, 1995). And, unlike the leisure aspect of contemplation, its restorative benefits have generated a noticeable amount of thought and research (see Ouellette, Heintzman, & Carette, 2005, for a partial review of this literature).

Spirituality and leisure

Paul Heintzman (2010) notes that interest in spirituality and leisure has gained considerable ground in recent years, a noticeable contrast to the weak interest in leisure and contemplation discussed in the preceding section. The areas where the spirituality–leisure link has been strongest are those centered on the leisure experience and include: therapeutic recreation, camping, recreational land management, outdoor recreation, tourism, and community recreation. He reviews some of the empirical research that has been conducted on this relationship, which has tended to concentrate on outdoor activities.

One conceptualization of spirituality and leisure is served up the idea of spiritual well-being. Prilleltensky & Prilleltensky (2006) offer the following definition:

> Spiritual well-being is a part of one's personal well-being, and relates to a sense of purpose and meaning in life. One who is spiritually engaged is able to make meaning out of values, feelings, thoughts, and actions, reconciling them with a higher being, mother nature, or another guiding light (p. 153).

Mosby's Dictionary of Complementary and Alternative Medicine (Jonas, 2005) adds that spiritual well-being is "a sense of peace and contentment stemming from an individual's relationship with the spiritual aspects of life."

Elsewhere, Heintzman (2002) has theorized that spiritual wellness may be thought of as a benefit of leisure. He argues that leisure experiences may consciously or unconsciously provide occasions for working

DOI: 10.1057/9781137569943.0007

through spiritual difficulties or even for becoming sensitized to the spiritual. In leisure, as free as it tends to be, there can be times when spirituality may be explored rather than repressed, as it sometimes is in more rigidly institutionalized settings (Heintzman, 2000).

As noted above both awe and enthrallment can be aroused while pursuing one or a few of NCAs. Both could also be emotional concomitants of a religious or nonreligious spirituality felt with reference to the natural environment. We know little about whether these spiritual experiences are likely to be casual leisure or one of the serious pursuits. That is, one can be deeply moved (in spiritual awe or enthrallment) by an intimate sexual experience, breathtaking view from a mountain top reached by helicopter, or live rendition of, say, Beethoven's "Ode to Joy," all being casual leisure activities. In the serious pursuits many an amateur astronomer spoke in research interviews about the absorbing experience in their NCA of "getting lost in space," accomplished while observing it with a good quality portable telescope (Stebbins, 1981). Furthermore, the same experience is possible in, for instance, such diverse serious activities as craftwork, artistic painting, choral singing (Liu & Stebbins, 2014), and chess (Puddephatt, 2003, pp. 272–278). Can project-based leisure generate enthrallment? There is no evidence on this question. Still the following sample of leisure projects could be as enthralling as their serious counterparts: genealogical research, disaster volunteering, acting in a community pageant, and giving an after-dinner speech.

Flow

Last but not least is the enthrallment found in flow (Csikszentmihalyi, 1990). Components 5, 7, and 8 can be understood as indicators of that emotion (see Chapter 1 of the present book). Much of the research on flow has been conducted on work activities, which, however, are by definition devotee pursuits. For after all, sense of competence and control (components 1 and 6) square nicely with the definition of devotee work also set out in Chapter 1 (see criteria 1 and 4).

Spirituality achieved through flow has been the subject of a handful of articles. For instance, Nelson & Rawlings (2007) observed a link between artistic creativity, spirituality, and flow felt while the creative experience was in process. Flinn (1995) found that her sample of country dancers experienced religious spirituality and flow while dancing. Purdy

DOI: 10.1057/9781137569943.0007

& Dupey (2005) have proposed a model of spiritual wellness, which includes the components of spirituality as engendered by flow.

Conclusion

The leisure-like nature of contemplation deserves closer consideration than the field of leisure studies has given it. Scholars there need to balance the problem-centered, instrumental orientation of attention restoration theory with theory and research on the intrinsic, leisure-like nature of contemplation as set out in types 2, 3, and 4. Here contemplation is both a process and a product endowed with immense value. Ouellette and Carette (2004), for example, underscore its importance for the elderly, arguing that contemplation is as important for them as physical, civic, and cultural activities.

In this respect Ouellette and Carette (2004) make a crucial point, namely, that it is important to find time for contemplation that leads to personal revitalization as achieved by getting to know oneself better. For them the monastery offers an ideal opportunity for reaching this goal. By the same token, however practical this quest may sometimes be, it is also likely to be experienced as leisure. For personal revitalization is very much akin to what is sometimes referred to in leisure studies as "re-creation." Through either process we get recharged to carry out life's obligatory activities. Meanwhile "getting to know oneself" relates closely to self-fulfillment, to learning what as individuals we are capable of, have an aptitude for, and have gained some background preparation to do. To be sure such learning is practical, but more importantly, it is also in the end the ultimate payoff of the various serious pursuits, in general, and the contemplation types 3 and 4, in particular.

The challenge for the individual, assuming that he or she seeks contemplation as a leisure pursuit of the sort just described, is to find time and place to do it. For many people in the hectic twenty-first century finding the time may well be the more difficult of these two. Contemplative time requires escape from disturbance, from jarring noise, distracting music, shouting people, blaring television sets, and a long list of other annoyances. For a multitude of city people these impediments are all too present in their everyday existence. For them, finding the time and the quiet and solitudinous places needed for effective, fulfilling contemplation will therefore require some substantial restructuring of

DOI: 10.1057/9781137569943.0007

that existence. Furthermore, to find such quiet and solitude, could well require the cooperation of particular others (e.g., friends, spouses, other family members). It could turn out to be more difficult to make these sorts of arrangements for contemplation for the purposes of leisure than for solving a difficult problem. The attraction of retreats for contemplation is evident here, whether for thinking through a problem or engaging in reflection or introspection as a leisure activity.

Spirituality, on the other hand, has generated considerably more interest in the study of leisure. The precise proportion in leisure of religious spirituality to the nonreligious kind, to my knowledge, has never been estimated. My sense of this highly scattered literature is that the two are about equally represented in it. Part of the problem in making such an estimate is that some people enthralled at the moment by a supernatural spirit may find it difficult to separate them, if indeed they even want to do so.

Contemplation and spirituality are personal, individual-oriented states of mind, while spirituality can also be a way of life. Altruism, the central emotion covered in the next chapter, is by contrast fully social.

Note

1 Paul Heintzman (personal communication, August 19, 2014) notes that the solitary contemplator on a retreat is often part of a larger group of participants who, when not alone, form into a temporary community on the site.

References

Aristotle (1915). *Ethica Nicomachea.* London: Oxford University Press.

Borrie, W., & Roggenbuck, J.W. (2001). The dynamic, emergent, and multi-phasic nature of on-site wilderness experiences. *Journal of Leisure Research*, 33, 202–228.

Csikszentmihalyi, M. (1990). *Flow: The psychology of optimal experience.* New York: Harper & Row.

Davidson, L., & Stebbins, R.A. (2011). *Serious leisure and nature: Sustainable consumption in the outdoors.* Houndmills, Basingstoke, UK: Palgrave Macmillan.

Doohan, L. (1990). *Leisure: A spiritual need*, Notre Dame, IN: Ave Maria Press.

DOI: 10.1057/9781137569943.0007

Flinn, J. (1995). American country dancing: A religious experience. *Journal of Popular Culture*, 29(1), 61–69.
de Grazia, S. (1962). *Of time, work, and leisure*. New York: Twentieth Century Fund.
Heintzman, P. (2000). Leisure and spiritual well-being relationships: A qualitative study. *Society and Leisure*, 23(1), 41–69.
Heintzman, P. (2002). A conceptual model of leisure and spiritual well-being. *Journal of Parks and Recreation Administration*, 20(4), 147–169.
Heintzman, P. (2010). Leisure studies and spirituality: A Christian critique. *Journal of the Christian Society for Kinesiology and Leisure Studies*, 1(1), 19–31.
Jonas, W.B. (2005). *Mosby's dictionary of complementary and alternative medicine*. Philadelphia, PA: Elsevier Mosby.
Kaplan, S. (1995) The restorative benefits of nature: Toward an integrative framework. *Journal of Environmental Psychology*, 15, 169–182.
Keltner, D., & Haidt, J. (2003). Approaching awe, a moral, spiritual, and aesthetic emotion. *Cognition and Emotion*, 17(2), 297–314.
Liu, H., & Stebbins, R.A. (2014). Concerted singing: Leisure fulfillment in a university faculty chorus. *Leisure Studies*, 33(5), 533–545.
Nelson, B., & Rawlings, D. (2007). Its own reward: A phenomenological study of artistic creativity. *Journal of Phenomenological Psychology*, 49(2), 95–106.
Neulinger, J. (1974). *The psychology of leisure: Research approaches to the study of leisure*. Springfield, IL: Charles C. Thomas.
Ouellette, P., & Carette, P. (2004). *Les motivations et les effets d'une retraite individuelle dans un monastère bénédictin*. Moncton, NB: École de Kinésiologie et de Récréologie, Université de Moncton.
Ouellette, P., Heintzman, P., & Carette, R. (2005). Motivations and effects of a retreat in a Benedictine monastery. In T. Delamere, C. Randall, & D. Robinson (Eds.), *The Eleventh Canadian Congress on Leisure Research. The Two Solitudes: Isolation or Impact*? (pp. 447–452). Nanaimo, BC: Department of Recreation and Tourism Management, Malaspina University-College. (Abstracts on CD-ROM).
Ouellette P., Kaplan, R., & Kaplan, S. (2005). The monastery as a restorative environment. *Journal of Environmental Psychology*, 25(2), 175–188.
Paddick, R.J. (1982). Time on my hands: Hands off my time. *Leisure Studies*, 1, 355–364.

DOI: 10.1057/9781137569943.0007

Parrott, W.G. (Ed.) (2001). *Emotions in social psychology: Key readings.* New York: Psychology Press.
Pieper, J. (1963). *Leisure: The basis of culture*, trans by A. Dru. New York: New American Library.
Prilleltensky, I., & Prilleltensky, O. (2006). *Promoting well-being: Linking personal, organizational, and community change.* Hoboken, NJ: John Wiley.
Puddephatt, A.J. (2003). Chess playing as strategic activity. *Symbolic Interaction,* 26, 263–284.
Purdy, M., & Dupey, P. (2005). Holistic flow model of spiritual wellness. *Counseling & Values,* 49(2), 95–106.
Stebbins, R.A. (1981). Science *amators*? Rewards and costs in amateur astronomy and archaeology. *Journal of Leisure Research*, 13(4), 289–304.
Stebbins, R.A. (1993). *Predicaments: Moral difficulty in everyday life.* Lanham, MD: University Press of America.
Stebbins, R.A. (2006). Contemplation as leisure and non-leisure. *Leisure Studies Association Newsletter*, 73(March), 21–23. (also available at www.seriousleisure.net/Digital Library, "Leisure Reflections No. 11").
Tanquerey, A.A. (1924). *Précis de théologie ascétique et mystique.* Paris: Desclé.

DOI: 10.1057/9781137569943.0007

5
Altruism

Abstract: *Altruism is a central component of volunteering, which is the main leisure activity in which this behavior/attitude is found. Voluntary altruism is the focus here, it being far more common than pure altruism. Quasi-volunteer altruism is also considered. Three distinct emotions are commonly aroused in altruistic behavior: compassion, generosity, and gratitude. Gratitude is a main reward, a kind of satisfaction that volunteers often look for from the target of their benefits. Eighteen theoretic types of volunteering as leisure are examined, followed by a discussion of a variety of community sectors that attract volunteer activity. Committees and boards of directors are discussed, after which the social worlds and the geographic spaces of volunteering are explored. The chapter ends with an examination of the careers available in career volunteering.*

Keywords: altruism; boards of directors; career; compassion; generosity; geographic space; gratitude; social world; volunteering

Stebbins, Robert A. *Leisure and Positive Psychology: Linking Activities with Positiveness.* Basingstoke: Palgrave Macmillan, 2015. DOI: 10.1057/9781137569943.0008.

 DOI: 10.1057/9781137569943.0008

Altruism is a central component of volunteering, which is the main leisure activity in which this behavior/attitude is found (see later definition). Although commonsense has it that volunteering is purely altruistic, both theory and data indicate that there is also a strong component of self-interest, or egotism, motivating it (Musick & Wilson, 2008, p. 65). This dual motivation must be recognized in any definition of altruism.

Hence, the first item on the agenda for this chapter is to define altruism. Next we consider three emotions that commonly accompany it: compassion, generosity, and gratitude. The volunteering in which altruism and these emotions are experienced is examined here as serious, casual, and project-based leisure. Volunteering is not always a wholly positive experience, which leads to a discussion of the social and spatial worlds of this activity where negativeness can sometimes dilute the satisfaction and fulfillment that is normally felt there. The chapter ends with a discussion of the serious volunteer's leisure career, itself a source of motivation.

Defining altruism

The guiding definition for this chapter is that of *voluntary altruism*. It has six defining qualities:

1 A mix of humane caring and sharing of oneself and one's resources;
2 at least a moderate freedom to chose the activity;
3 a lack of coercion from biophysical, biosocial, or socially compelling forces;
4 a sensitivity to certain needs and wants of a target of benefits;
5 an expectation of little or no remuneration or payment in kind; and
6 an expectation of receiving some sort of satisfaction for action undertaken on behalf of the target (from Smith, Stebbins, & Dover, 2006, pp. 238–239).

The sixth quality recognizes the role of self-interest, or egotism, in volunteering. The second and third qualities refer to the leisure-like nature of this activity.

Voluntary altruism differs from *pure altruism*. The latter (sometimes known as "absolute altruism") is an ideal form of altruism that is very rarely achieved in humans, imperfect as they are. In it the altruistic

DOI: 10.1057/9781137569943.0008

person is totally focused on helping and satisfying another person, group, or other target of benefits, doing so without any sense of self-satisfaction from the altruistic act (Smith, Stebbins, & Dover, 2006, p. 19). The satisfaction found in an altruistic act might be, for example, feeling good about being altruistic as a socially valued trait or act, enjoying the satisfaction of the person helped, and helping the target of benefits gain some satisfaction from the act. Nevertheless, the pure altruist would never experience this positive feature of volunteering.

Finally, to put these two definitions in perspective, consider *quasi-volunteer altruism*. It is the kind of voluntary altruism that is expressed in under-remunerated activity. Whether an activity is under-remunerated or fairly remunerated is determined by labor market prices for the service rendered (Smith, Stebbins, & Dover, 2006, p. 19).

Altruism and its emotions

From one angle voluntary altruism is prosocial behavior, whereas from another it is an attitude. That is, such altruism is, among things, a stable tendency to care for others and to be sensitive to their needs (see qualities 1 and 4 above). When we put this tendency into action, we are engaging in altruistic behavior. Altruism is a main plank in the platform of positive psychology (Snyder, Lopez, & Pedrotti, 2011, chapter 11).

Altruistic behavior arouses three distinct emotions, one of which is *compassion*. Eric Cassell (2009) holds that compassion is experienced when one sees another suffering through serious troubles that are not self-inflicted and that the first also senses might be experienced personally. Troubles that are not self-inflicted result from an "unjust fate," such as war, murder, mayhem, unprovoked violence, natural disaster, and the like. Some of these calamitous situations trigger through compassion in people outside them a desire to volunteer, to help in some way. This occurs in substantial part because the volunteer can identify, or empathize, with the suffering target of this compassion. By acting on this emotion we give concrete expression to the prosocial element in altruism. Parrott (2001) classifies compassion as a tertiary emotion, placing it in the same category as that of caring.

Expressing *generosity* results in the same interhuman connection, albeit accomplished from a somewhat different angle. As an emotion (Robinson, 2009) it is aroused by a desire to help in some particular way

DOI: 10.1057/9781137569943.0008

using one's resources magnanimously. Here volunteers typically help by giving to the target of benefits their time, effort, or money or other goods (e.g., food, clothing, tools). This is done in the spirit of goodwill in an atmosphere of negligible coercion. As for *gratitude* it is, when conceived of with reference to volunteering, a main reward, a kind of satisfaction that volunteers often look for from the target of their benefits. This is one of many aspects of the self-interested (egotistic) side of the altruistic/self-interested equation, which distinguishes volunteering from the other serious pursuits (see above quality no. 6 in the definition of voluntary altruism).

Volunteering as leisure

Having set out in Chapter 1 the definitions of volunteer and volunteering that guide discussion in this book, the time has come to examine more closely the manifestation of these two in the three forms of leisure. Volitionally speaking, volunteer activities are motivated, in part, by one of six types of interest: interest in activities involving (1) people, (2) ideas, (3) things, (4) flora, (5) fauna, (6) the natural environment, or a combination of these (Stebbins, 2007/2015). Each type or combination of types offers its volunteers an opportunity to pursue through an altruistic activity a particular kind of interest. Thus, volunteers interested in working with certain ideas are attracted to idea-based volunteering, while those interested in certain kinds of animals are attracted to faunal volunteering. Interest forms the first dimension of a typology of volunteers and volunteering.

But, since volunteers and volunteering cannot be explained by interest alone, a second dimension is needed. This is supplied by the SLP and its three forms. This perspective, as already noted, sets out the motivational and contextual (sociocultural, historical) foundation of the three. The intersections of these two dimensions result in 18 types of volunteers and volunteering, exemplified in idea-based serious leisure volunteering, material casual leisure volunteering (working with things), and environmental project-based volunteering (see Table 5.1).

These types are, however, rather general; they are theoretic constructions. By contrast, actual volunteers prefer to channel their altruistic leisure toward a particular sector of community life. Here they seek careers in serious leisure volunteering either through formal activity – working within

DOI: 10.1057/9781137569943.0008

TABLE 5.1 *Types of Volunteers and Volunteering*

	Type of Volunteer		
Leisure Interest	**Serious Leisure (SL)**	**Casual Leisure (CL)**	**Project-Based Leisure (PBL)**
Popular	SL Popular	CL Popular	PBL Popular
Idea-Based	SL Idea-Based	CL Idea-Based	PBL Idea-Based
Material	SL Material	CL Material	PBL Material
Floral	SL Floral	CL Floral	PBL Floral
Faunal	SL Faunal	CL Faunal	PBL Faunal
Environmental	SL Environmental	CL Environmental	PBL Environmental

Source: Stebbins (2007/2015).

an organization or association – or through informal activity – working with friends or neighbors, or working with a small collectivity such as a club or self-help group. Some volunteer careers combine both types. These community sectors also offer abundant opportunity for casual and project-based volunteering. Elsewhere (Stebbins, 2014, chapter 5) I consider 18 sectors, among them, health, politics, religion, science, education, and the natural environment.

Committees and boards

Committee work and the work of boards of directors are two common kinds of volunteering; they are found in all the aforementioned sectors. Some committee work consists of casual volunteering (such activity defined as nonwork obligation is not volunteering), as in a group of musicians who set the stage for a concert to be given by their community orchestra or the set of volunteers who agree to serve refreshments at the annual general meeting of their nonprofit organization. The sense of altruism is alive here, and it probably outweighs that of self-interest. Generosity and gratitude are also evident in such situations.

Other committees, however, are the scene of serious volunteer activity. Here knowledge, experience and, possibly, skill are required for effective

DOI: 10.1057/9781137569943.0008

participation. A nonprofit's finance committee is a common example (where its treasurer cannot also take on this function). A committee established to plan for its future is another. Often, it appears, members of these little groups gain most of their relevant knowledge and experience on the job; their taste and talent for the committee's terms of reference being sufficient for recruitment to it. This is career volunteering in that it is serious leisure, even though normally membership in such groups lasts only a few years. Consequently, the sense of a career as experienced in growing fulfillment is truncated, especially when the term of membership is so short. In sum, we might qualify such activity as marginal career volunteering, notwithstanding that it is volunteering of considerable importance for the organization.

For volunteers serving in nonprofit organizations, the possibility exists of achieving some even loftier volunteer roles, namely, those constituting the group's board of directors (trustees). This is a special kind of career volunteering found in all nonprofit groups that organize amateur, hobbyist, or volunteer activities. The chair of the board lies at the top of this short though elite hierarchy, while being elected treasurer or secretary is also an honor (and a major responsibility). The rest of the board also basks in the prestige of having been elected to it, which puts them in a position to see their nonprofit from an unusual top-down angle.

Note that, to staff their boards of directors, nonprofit organizations in the arts and hobbies draw on volunteers from among their members. Thus, the board of a model railroad club is composed of elected hobbyist members, while that of a community theater is formed from its elected amateur actors. Often, this stint of career volunteering is short, since normally directors and officers of these groups are legally allowed to serve in this capacity for one or two terms only. Rare is the amateur or hobbyist activity that also offers a long volunteer career, as pursued through an evolved bureaucratic structure, often one operating on a national or international level. A main example of this formation is evident in the international communities of male and female barbershop singers (Stebbins, 1996). With this exception, and possibly a handful of others, these career volunteers on boards of directors simultaneously pursue their amateur or hobbyist passion, returning to it with unadulterated attention once no longer being eligible to serve on "the executive" (or for personal reasons leave before this).

Where a long career is evident in career volunteering as realized through board membership is among that small number of citizens in

DOI: 10.1057/9781137569943.0008

the community who pursue over the years successive memberships on different boards. Research data on these dedicated enthusiasts is scarce. My own experience as one of them and my informal observations of like-minded volunteers in the city of Calgary suggest that they do exist and that their contributions to the community are noteworthy. In my case I participated at different times in four boards serving the city's francophones, two of which directed immigrant-welcoming organizations and two of which directed general French-community groups. Are there not, also in the large cities in the West, career volunteers of this bent – community leaders – who, depending on taste, talent, and experience, serve on the boards of, among others, a string of arts, sports, or community service organizations?

Altruism in action

Serious leisure volunteering is most accurately referred to as "career volunteering," primarily because, as in the other serious pursuits, participants can see themselves getting better at what they do. In this regard, it is appears that the motive of self-interestedness drives the pursuit of such a career at least as much as the motive of altruism. This even holds where altruism inspired a person to enter the field in the first place. A main reason for this difference is that career volunteering involves acquiring, over time, certain skills, knowledge, or training and, not infrequently, two or three of these. Their acquisition contributes to the sense of an evolving career, itself highly rewarding. As Coralie McCormack and her colleagues (2008) summed it up for female baby boomers who were seeking this kind of volunteering in retirement, "I want to do more than just cut the sandwiches."

Volunteering often carries with it a clear obligation to be at a particular place, at a specified time, to perform a certain function. Yet career volunteering seems to engender no greater load of commitments than many other serious leisure pursuits. For example, serious leisure participants can be obligated to attend rehearsals and perform in the next concert of the community orchestra, play for their team in an upcoming game in the local industrial baseball league, or, as career volunteers, go to the neighborhood primary school at four o'clock two days a week to help children with reading problems.

Moreover, as with other types of serious leisure, career volunteering brings on the occasional need to persevere. Participants who want to

DOI: 10.1057/9781137569943.0008

continue experiencing the same level of satisfaction in the activity have to meet certain challenges from time to time. Thus, musicians must practice assiduously to master difficult musical passages, baseball players must throw repeatedly to perfect their favorite pitches, and some volunteers must search their imaginations for new approaches with which to help children with reading problems. Perseverance can also help volunteers realize such rewards as self-actualization and self-expression. It happens in all three types of serious leisure that the deepest rewards sometimes come at the end of the activity, rather than during it.

Volunteers serving in a nonprofit organization usually perform tasks delegated to them by a superior. This person is normally either a paid employee (a manager) or a senior volunteer in the same organization. Superiors believe these are tasks that volunteers can do, given adequate training and experience, tasks that the staff believes are beyond their jurisdiction or, given budgetary limitations, believes they cannot take on themselves.

Such arrangements turn these volunteers into outsiders in agencies and nonprofit organizations otherwise composed of insiders. Indeed, the volunteers' expertise and competence may even threaten some insiders. All this indicates that organizational volunteers are neither facsimiles of professionals, as amateurs are, nor bureaucratized workers. Instead, they are often a special class of helper in someone else's occupational world.

Some areas of career volunteering require significant amounts of training. Indeed some, including many in education, require full certification of the volunteer, even though this person is working without pay. Obviously, these areas are open only to specialists who have retired or who find their work too exciting to abandon in their free time after work. Yet, it is fortunate that entry into the large majority of volunteer activities is substantially less restrictive.

It is also obvious that some of the activities just discussed lend themselves to either casual involvement or serious involvement, depending on the activities offered to the volunteer. For instance, a clear difference exists in the ability and experience required to coordinate a canoe race consisting of scores of contestants and that required to ensure that each pair of paddlers is properly registered. The first exemplifies career volunteering, whereas the second is an instance of casual volunteering. But, clearly, both types of volunteering are often needed if an event or service is be carried out effectively.

DOI: 10.1057/9781137569943.0008

In short, casual volunteering can be absolutely crucial to a larger volunteer project or activity, even when it requires only minimal skill, knowledge, or experience. And, as such, it can be satisfying leisure for the participant. Yet, this satisfaction differs profoundly from the fulfillment found in career volunteering. The latter comes from experiencing the special rewards exclusively available in all three types of serious leisure, rewards unavailable in casual volunteering, in particular, or in casual leisure, in general.

Social worlds in volunteering

It was observed in Chapter 1 that every social world contains four types of members identified by David Unruh (1979; 1980) as strangers, tourists, regulars, and insiders. The strangers are intermediaries who normally participate little in the leisure/work activity itself, but who nonetheless do something important to make it possible. Most strangers in volunteering function as volunteer coordinators or executive directors employed by nonprofit organizations or as team directors in, for example, disaster volunteering. The tourists are temporary participants in a social world; they have come on the scene momentarily for entertainment, diversion, profit, or other benefits. The target of benefits served by most volunteers may be classified here. The former are the recipients of the latter's altruistic activities and generous giving of time and effort. The former are also inclined to express their gratitude to the latter for helping them.

The regulars routinely participate in the social world; in the serious pursuits, they are the amateurs, hobbyists, and volunteers themselves. Many volunteers serve with or meet up with others engaging in the same or related activities. Members of committees and boards of directors exemplify this arrangement. Volunteers working in teams in disaster relief, search and rescue, arts festivals, sports events, self-help groups, and so on, rub elbows with co-participants. These occasions can generate attachment and respect for them as well as the satisfaction that comes from pleasing social interaction. People who serve alone, as do mentors, tutors, children's storytellers, street-corner solicitors, and those who work individually with the handicapped miss out on this feature of the volunteer's social world.

The insiders are those among the participants who show exceptional devotion to the social world they share, to maintaining it, to advancing it.

DOI: 10.1057/9781137569943.0008

Among volunteers such enthusiasts stand out in, for instance, boards of directors, volunteer fire-fighting units, self-help groups, and the Guardian Angels (a nonviolent volunteer organization dedicated to restoring order to urban streets and transportation systems). In the SLP such people are analyzed according to an involvement scale as either "core devotees" or "moderate devotees" and contrasted with "participants" (Stebbins, 2014, chapter 2; see also www.seriousleisure.net/SLP Diagrams).

The spaces of volunteering

Leisure space conceived of in geographic terms has conventionally referred to the locations where leisure activities are pursued. These spaces may be natural or artificial or a combination of both. And nowadays they may be virtual. David Crouch summarizes the importance of understanding leisure in terms of geographic space thus conceived of:

> Leisure happens, is produced in spaces. These spaces may be material, and related to concrete locations. Yet the spaces, and therefore geographies, of leisure may be metaphorical, even imaginative. Imaginative spaces are not merely in the virtual space of contemporary nature but also in the imagination of consumer and the representations of the agencies providing in producing leisure sites: visual culture and other narratives of communication.... Space, then, can be important in metaphorically "shaping," contextualizing leisure and commercial and public policy prefiguring of the meaning of leisure sites, and the leisure experience may be transformed by the way in which individuals encounter those spaces and activities. (Crouch, 2006, p. 127)

In the language of this book, volunteer and other leisure activities also occur in geographic space as just described. This context helps shape those activities and gives them meaning for the individual participant.

As Crouch's words imply, geographic analysis usually focuses on leisure in general. Yet, there are also particular ways in which geographic space is used and these ways vary according to the kind of activity engaged in. This more focused line of analysis is relatively new (see Stebbins, 2013), and has furthermore only been developed for the serious pursuits. Still, we can profit from an informative new slant on leisure and positive psychology accomplished by examining how space influences the volunteer experience.

Of the seven types of space identified by Stebbins, the one he labeled "helping" space directly concerns volunteers. This is the space within

DOI: 10.1057/9781137569943.0008

which help is provided. The help may be that of either volunteers or professionals, with the latter being classified here as devotee workers. Among the second the offices of counselors and consultants serve as a main space within which they pursue their core activities. Other spaces for some of this group's core activities may include a home office, a public or institutional library, and a specialized book store or website.

Career volunteers also have their distinctive spaces. These are evident to some extent by where they serve, as in a zoo or museum, on a board of directors (board room or equivalent), at a primary school, or at a hospital. The main space for volunteers whose core activity is to preserve or maintain the natural environment is a river, forest, or town park as well as the air they breathe and the surrounding terrain on which they function. Recreational volunteers serve in spaces such as camps, sports centers, municipal recreational facilities, and sites for sporting competitions (e.g., gymnasia, swimming pools, ski hills, running courses).

The work/leisure spaces, the helping spaces included, are perceivable by way of some or all of the following spatial properties: visual, olfactory, tactile, and auditory (including little or no sound). That is, they are available to us through our senses. And through these senses those spaces take on special meaning, in particular, as "places" (Elkington, 2014) where, in career volunteering for example, self-fulfillment is found. Thus, a volunteer with the ski patrol not only loves skiing but also loves in the mountain environment within which this activity is carried out. The space where the nonprofit board meets is also a place for its members, who make important organizationally related decisions there surrounded by its diverse accoutrements (e.g., pictures, posters, windows, refreshment facilities, electronic equipment, and file cabinets) as well as such climatic features as temperature, quality of air, and noisy ventilators.

All this is part of the experience of volunteering in and expressing altruism through its many roles. This is where compassion and generosity are operationalized, as it were. Moreover, not all of these experiences are wholly positive, for the board room may be consistently too hot or too cold, the ventilator too noisy, the conditions of the ski hill most unpleasant (from cold or wind), and the like. Nonetheless, as noted earlier, the serious pursuits are never completely positive. Participants must from time to time persevere through an assortment of difficulties. Conquering this adversity is indeed part of the fulfillment they feel as their career in the pursuit continues over the years.

DOI: 10.1057/9781137569943.0008

Careers in career volunteering

A career in any serious pursuit is, at its subjective level, a significant motivator. Most broadly put, the sense of getting better at the core activities that comprise the pursuit (i.e., gaining ever more knowledge, experience, and skill) inspires the participant to continue on this path to personal development. Stebbins (2014, chapter 5) presents a lengthy exposition of the careers available in career volunteering. In general, he analyzes these careers according to their four or five stages: beginning, development, establishment, maintenance, and where it occurs, decline (see also Chapter 1 of this book). Casual and project-based volunteers are considered in this discussion, though only to the extent that their activities sometimes put them on the road to serious leisure volunteering.

In any case there is in most volunteering a strong sense of altruism toward the target of benefits that motivates initial participation, with self-interest becoming the more dominant attitude later in the volunteer's career (see Gage III & Thapa, 2012). Nonetheless, Holmes (2001, p. 108) showed in her study of museum volunteers that personal interests motivate them even at the onset of their fulfillment careers. Thus, they may have an interest in the museum itself or one of its collections or they may want to "give something back to the institution." Green & Chalip (2004) found in their study of volunteers at the Sydney Olympic Games such self-interested motives as wanting to help the event or the community, have a learning experience, or just get in on the excitement.

Conclusion

The study of volunteers and volunteering as participants in a leisure activity tends to accent the individual and what this person gains from it and gives to the target of benefits. This slant is consistent with that of mainstream psychology, in that the analytic center rests on the person. The SLP, however, with its propositions about the context of leisure activities, also takes us beyond this individualistic focus to the contributions that volunteers (and participants in the other serious pursuits) can make to the larger social entities, notably, organizations, local communities, and entire societies.

This extension into the domain of positive sociology (Stebbins, 2009, see especially chapter 6) is evident in modern positive psychology. For

DOI: 10.1057/9781137569943.0008

example, Lopez & Snyder (2009, Part 9) offer five chapters on positive institutions, while Snyder, Lopez, & Pedrotti (2011, chapter 17) write about building better communities through the "me/we balance." Linley, Harrington, & Garcea (2013) collection is devoted to positive psychology and work. Chapter 6 shows how this scholarly overlap works where leisure is the common ground.

References

Cassell, E.J. (2009). Compassion. In S.J. Lopez & C.R. Snyder (Eds.), *The Oxford handbook of positive psychology* (pp. 393–403). New York: Oxford University Press.

Crouch, D. (2006). Geographies of leisure. In C. Rojek, S.M. Shaw, & A.J. Veal (Eds.), *A handbook of leisure studies* (pp. 125–139). Houndmills, UK: Palgrave Macmillan.

Elkington, S. (2014). Sites of serious leisure: Acting up in space and place. In S. Elkington & S. Gammon (Eds.), *Leisure in mind: Meaning, motives, and learning* (pp. 93–111). London: Routledge.

Gage III, R., & Thapa, B. (2012). Volunteer motivations and constraints among college students: Analysis of the volunteer function inventory and leisure constraints models. *Nonprofit and Voluntary Sector Quarterly*, 41, 405–430.

Green, B., & Chalip, L. (2004). Paths to volunteer commitment: Lessons from the Sydney Olympic Games. In R.A. Stebbins & M. Graham (Eds.), *Volunteering as leisure/leisure as volunteering: An international assessment* (pp. 49–68). Wallingford, UK: CABI.

Holmes, K. (2001). The motivation and retention of front-house volunteers at museum and heritage attractions. In M. Graham & M. Foley (Eds.), *Leisure volunteering: Marginal or inclusive?* (pp. 95–110). Eastbourne, UK: Leisure Studies Association, LSA Publication No. 75.

Linley, P.A., Harrington, S., & Garcea, N. (Eds.) (2013). *The Oxford handbook of positive psychology and work*. New York: Oxford University Press.

Lopez, S.J., & Snyder, C.R. (2009). *The Oxford handbook of positive psychology*, 2nd ed. New York: Oxford University Press.

McCormack, C., Cameron, P., Campbell, A., & Pollock, K. (2008). I want to do more than just cut the sandwiches: Female baby boomers

seek authentic leisure in retirement. *Annals of Leisure Research*, 11, 145–167.
Musick, M.A., & Wilson, J. (2008). *Volunteers: A social profile*. Bloomington, IN: Indiana University Press.
Parrott, W.G. (Ed.) (2001). *Emotions in social psychology: Key readings*. New York: Psychology Press.
Robinson, D.L. (2009). Brain function, mental experience and personality. *The Netherlands Journal of Psychology*, 64, 152–167.
Smith, D.H., Stebbins, R.A., & Dover, M. (2006). *A dictionary of nonprofit terms and concepts*. Bloomington, IN: Indiana University Press.
Snyder, C.R., Lopez, S.J., & Pedrotti, J.T. (2011). *Positive psychology: The scientific and practical explorations of human strengths*, 2nd ed. Thousand Oaks, CA: Sage.
Stebbins, R.A. (1996). *The barbershop singer: Inside the social world of a musical hobby*. Toronto, ON: University of Toronto Press.
Stebbins, R.A. (2007/2015). *Serious leisure: A perspective for our time*. New Brunswick, NJ: Transaction. (Paperback edition with new Preface, 2015).
Stebbins, R.A. (2009). *Personal decisions in the public square: Beyond problem solving into a positive sociology*. New Brunswick, NJ: Transaction.
Stebbins, R.A. (2013). The spaces of the serious pursuits: A typology. *Leisure Studies Association Newsletter*, 95 (July), 21–24 (also available at www.seriousleisure.net/Digital Library, "Leisure Reflections No. 33").
Stebbins, R.A. (2014). *Careers in serious leisure: From dabbler to devotee in search of fulfillment*. Houndmills, UK: Palgrave Macmillan.
Unruh, D.R. (1979). Characteristics and types of participation in social worlds. *Symbolic Interaction*, 2, 115–130.
Unruh, D.R. (1980). The nature of social worlds. *Pacific Sociological Review*, 23, 271–296.

DOI: 10.1057/9781137569943.0008

6

Contributions to Community and Organization

Abstract: *When it comes to contributions to community and organization, generosity is the principal emotion. Altruism is also strongly felt during such activity. Community involvement is the process by which volunteers, amateurs, and hobbyists can contribute to collective life. A broader sort of community involvement (sometimes also carried out on a regional or societal level) comes from pursuing volunteer activities, which may be enacted as serious, casual, or project-based leisure. This, the most common conception of community involvement, is often discussed as civil labor. Civil labor, however conceived of, generates social capital. In leisure, as in most other areas of life, many activities are structured, or organized, in small groups, social networks, and grassroots organizations as well as in larger complex organizations and still more broadly, in tribes, social worlds, and social movements. The chapter ends with an examination of caring and community involvement.*

Keywords: altruism; amateurs; caring; civil labor; community; generosity; hobbyists; organizations; volunteers

Stebbins, Robert A. *Leisure and Positive Psychology: Linking Activities with Positiveness.* Basingstoke: Palgrave Macmillan, 2015. DOI: 10.1057/9781137569943.0009.

DOI: 10.1057/9781137569943.0009

Being generous with time, effort, and, for some benefactors, money reveals the principal emotion in this area of positive psychology. As in all voluntary action altruism is also strongly felt when volunteers contribute to the community. That said, volunteers (career and casual) are not the only contributors to community life – interpreted here to include national and international communities – for many amateurs hobbyists, and participants in projects do the same, albeit leavening their altruism with a strong flavoring of self-interestedness.

Since generosity and altruism were examined in detail in the preceding chapter, they need no further explication in the present one. Rather here, by drawing on the ideas of civil labor and social capital, we will show how these two positive emotions contribute to community life. To the extent that they have a social base, all the serious pursuits have this effect. The contribution to community through caring is also discussed.

Community involvement

Most generally put, community involvement is the process by which volunteers, amateurs, and hobbyists can contribute to collective life. Such involvement is defined as:

> local voluntary action, where members of a local community participate together in nonprofit groups or in other community activities. Often the goal here is to improve community life. This concept, which is synonymous with those of civic, civil, citizen, and grassroots involvement, is broader than that of "citizen participation," in that it includes both local political voluntary action and non-political voluntary action. (Smith, Stebbins, & Dover, 2006, p. 52)

According to this definition, the goal is often to improve communal life. Often, yes, but not invariably. For, as will become apparent shortly, a number of leisure activities do not have as their goal such improvement, even if, at times, some of them realize it anyway.

Leisure through community involvement

Much of what has been written in the past under this heading has borne on the contributions serious leisure enthusiasts make to the social and cultural enrichment of their local community. This kind of community

DOI: 10.1057/9781137569943.0009

involvement is evident when, for example, the town's civic orchestra provides it every three or four months with a concert of classical music or the local astronomy society offers an annual "star night" during which the public may observe the heavens using the telescopes of club members. And model railroaders in the area sometimes mount for popular consumption exhibitions of the fruits of their hobby. Lyons and Dionigi (2007) found, in a study of older Australian adults in Masters sport, that, through their participation there, they feel a sense of "giving something back" to the community. Furthermore, Hemingway (1999) and Reid (1995) have argued that, when considering leisure's contribution to community, it is important to distinguish between different kinds of activities. The examples above – all of them serious leisure – illustrate contributions quite distinct from those made through the casual and project-based forms.

A broader sort of community involvement (sometimes also carried out on a regional or societal level) comes from pursuing volunteer activities, which may be enacted as serious, casual, or project-based leisure. This is the most common conception of "community involvement," which is often discussed as *civil labor*. Such "labor" has members of a local community participating together as volunteers in nonprofit groups or other community activities. On this level a principal intention is to improve community life. Civil labor, which is broadly synonymous with community involvement, differs mainly in emphasis; the stress is on human activity devoted to unpaid renewal and expansion of social capital (Rojek, 2002, p. 21).

Rojek (2002, pp. 26–27) argues that, for the most part, civil labor consists of the community contribution made by amateurs, hobbyists, and career volunteers when they pursue their serious leisure. This is precisely what Leadbeater and Miller (2004) have in mind in their book about how amateurs in various fields are shaping the twenty-first-century economy and society in the West. Helft (2007) offers a concrete example in an article about amateur mapmakers, who using simple Internet tools are reshaping online map services and offering viewers far more detail of many more geographic sites than heretofore.

Civil labor, however conceived of, generates *social capital* defined here, following Putnam (2000, p. 19), as the links among individuals manifested in social networks, trustworthiness, acts motivated by the norm of reciprocity, and the like that develop in a community or larger society. The term is an analogy to the concepts of human capital and physical

DOI: 10.1057/9781137569943.0009

capital (e.g., financial resources, natural resources); it emphasizes that human groups of all kinds also benefit from and advance their interests according to the salutary interrelations of their members. Community involvement also generates social capital, but as already noted, it includes amateur and hobbyist activities, where this result, though it occurs, is not their primary purpose.

Self-interestedness also dominates nearly all other casual leisure, the glaring exception being, of course, casual volunteering. It is done expressly as civil labor. And, in the process of doing it, volunteers may well meet and serve with people never before encountered. So we must conclude, contrary to Rojek, that such labor is not limited to serious leisure, but finds its place in the volunteer type of casual leisure as well.

Moreover, volunteer project-based leisure may be conceived of as civil labor. Project-based leisure has potential in at least two ways for building community. First, it too can bring into contact people who otherwise have no reason to meet, or at least meet frequently. Second, by way of event volunteering and other short-term, collective altruistic activity, it can contribute to carrying out community events and projects. In other words, some project-based leisure (mostly one-shot volunteer projects, it appears) can also be conceived of as civil labor as just defined, suggesting that such activity can be other than serious leisure. In fact, the mountain hobbyists studied by the author (Stebbins, 2005) occasionally rounded out their leisure lifestyles by sporadically undertaking or participating in (typically volunteer) projects of this nature.

Clearly, to constitute community involvement, leisure must be collective in some fashion; the reclusive hobbies and amateur activities (e.g., liberal arts, some amateur piano and guitar) fail to qualify. Furthermore, when it comes to social capital, as opposed to civil labor and community involvement, I do not believe a case exists for privileging any of the three forms of leisure as the principal or most important way of generating the former. What is important is that people come together in voluntary action, as motivated by voluntary altruism, doing so long enough to learn something about one another, learn to trust one another (where experience warrants), develop "other-regarding" or altruistic love for one another (Jeffries et al., 2006), and for these reasons become willing to continue their interaction. True, many forms of serious leisure encourage sustained contact capable of fostering such learning, as seen in routine participation in many volunteer emergency services, hobbyist clubs, and arts and sports groups. Project leisure can also be a source of

DOI: 10.1057/9781137569943.0009

social capital, though here, such capital is of more limited scope than that generated through the long-term serious pursuits.

As for casual leisure volunteering, it may be short term or long term. Here people are sometimes joined in such leisure with strangers, especially these days over the Internet. The same happens with *tribes*: fragmented groupings left over from the preceding era of mass consumption, groupings recognized today by their unique tastes, lifestyles, and form of social organization (Maffesoli, 1996). Maffesoli identifies and describes this postmodern phenomenon, which spans national borders. In this regard, he observes that mass culture has disintegrated, leaving in its wake a diversity of tribes, including the followers of heavy metal music and those youth who participate in raves. Tribes are special leisure organizations, special ways of organizing the pursuit of particular kinds of casual leisure. Tribes are also found in serious leisure, but not, however, in project-based leisure (see Stebbins, 2002, pp. 69–71).

Contribution to organizations

In leisure, as in most other areas of life, many activities are structured, or organized, in small groups, social networks, and grassroots organizations as well as in larger complex organizations and still more broadly, in tribes, social worlds, and social movements (Stebbins, 2002). Each structures the social behavior of its members in particular ways, some of those ways being unique to that kind of organization. And, as stated earlier, individual interests also structure the organizational entities that facilitate these interests, which includes establishing those entities in the first place. Here the positive role of human agency is again evident. Thus we may say about leisure organizations, as with other kinds of organizations, that participation in them amounts to a two-way street of influence running from individual to collectivity and the reverse. This is the first of three critical assumptions on which this discussion of leisure and organization is based.

The second critical assumption is that members of the different sorts of organizations (defined below in the wide sense of social organization) know they are members. Third, such people value highly their membership for, given that we are considering only leisure organizations entered without coercion, members would abandon them were they substantially disvalued. Moreover, when they are highly valued, belonging itself

DOI: 10.1057/9781137569943.0009

becomes an important motive, since membership enables pursuit of one or more of the leisure activities the organization promotes and facilitates and its members are eager to pursue. Yet it should be clear that belonging to any of these organizational entities, even when centered on leisure, is never wholly a positive experience; for example, spouses have their tiffs, dissension shakes up some groups, ideological tensions can splinter a social movement, and so on.

Let us note before going further into the matter of the organization of leisure that many leisure activities in all three forms also appear to allow for, if not require, solitary participation, volunteering being the chief exception. Thus, someone may, in solitude, play the piano or the guitar, collect rocks or seashells, sit and daydream, or assemble a complicated electronic device from a kit. Volunteering, however, is inherently organizational in the broad sense of the word, since by definition, it involves directly or indirectly serving other people, be they individuals or groups. What, then, do I mean by "the broad sense" of the concept of organization?

"Organization" is used here as shorthand for the range of collectivities mentioned at the start of this section (dyads to social movements) that add social and psychological structure to leisure life. Accordingly, discussion in this section will center primarily on these different types manifested as leisure organizations rather than on the community or societal organization of leisure, as seen in the sweeping communal arrangements that make available leisure services and opportunities. Additionally, the present chapter requires only an *aperçu* of the different kinds of organization common in leisure, with a fuller treatment of them being available elsewhere (Stebbins, 2002).

Types of organizations

So, in harmony with what was said in Chapter 3 about positive relationships, note that some leisure is pursued in dyads (e.g., two friends organizing a surprise birthday party for someone or going together to the cinema). The triad is also a recognizable arrangement within which to partake of leisure (e.g., three people on a fishing trip, a classical music trio), and the same holds for the small, primary group (e.g., church basketball team, several friends who routinely hike together, four couples who dine monthly at a restaurant). These three types of organization are

DOI: 10.1057/9781137569943.0009

found in all three forms of leisure. The emotions of acceptance, love, sympathy, and admiration/respect are, where appropriate, expressed in these organizations.

Turning to the social network the definition that best fits the small amount of work done on this form of organization within the domain of leisure is Elizabeth Bott's (1957, p. 59). Hers is simple: a social network is "a set of social relationships for which there is no common boundary." In the strict sense of the word, a network is not a structure, since it has no shared boundaries (boundaries recognized by everyone in the structure), no commonly recognized hierarchy, and no central coordinating agency. Nevertheless, links exist between others in the network, in that some members are directly in touch with each other while other members are not.

As individuals pursue their leisure interests, they commonly develop networks of friends and acquaintances related in one way or another to these interests. When a person acquires more such interests, the number of networks tends to grow accordingly, bearing in mind, however, that members of some of these will sometimes overlap. For instance, a few members of John's dog breeding network – they might be suppliers, veterinarians, or other breeders – are also members of his golf network – which would probably include (golf-related) suppliers, course personnel, and other golfers. Knowing about people's leisure networks helps explain how they, fired by positive agency, socially organize their leisure time.

At the next level of organization – the grassroots association – serious leisure predominates, while some manifestations of it can also be found in casual leisure. The very nature of project-based leisure would seem to preclude grassroots associations from emerging around this form. According to Smith (2000, p. 8):

> grassroots associations are locally based, significantly autonomous, volunteer-run formal nonprofit (i.e., voluntary) groups that manifest substantial voluntary altruism as groups and use the associational form of organization and, thus, have official memberships of volunteers who perform most, and often all, of the work/activity done in and by these nonprofits.

The term "formal" in this definition refers in fact to a scale of structure and operations that, in an actual association, may be informal, semi-formal, or formal. Moreover, the line separating grassroots associations from paid-staff voluntary groups – treated in the next paragraph as volunteer organizations – is unavoidably fuzzy, distinguishing the two

DOI: 10.1057/9781137569943.0009

being primarily a matter of gradation. Both types fall under the heading of *voluntary groups*: "nonprofit groups of any type, whether grassroots associations or based on paid staff, and whether local, national, or international in scope" (Smith, 2000, p. ix). Formal grassroots associations include such entities as Girl Guide troops, stamp collectors' societies, singles' clubs, outlaw biker gangs, and college fraternities and sororities. By contrast, self-help, friendship, and book-discussion groups, for example, are often informal.

Turning to volunteer organizations, they offer leisure only to career and casual volunteers and to volunteers serving on projects. Volunteer organizations are distinguished by their reliance on paid staff, and by the fact that they are established to facilitate work for a cause or provision of a service rather than pursuit of a pastime. They nonetheless depend significantly on volunteer help to reach their objectives.

Pearce (1993, p. 15) holds that by far the largest number of volunteers work in these organizations. Yet some volunteer organizations may be staffed entirely by remunerated employees, volunteers only being engaged as unpaid members of their boards of directors. Hospitals and universities present two main examples. Many foundations can be similarly classified. Other volunteer organizations have a more even mix of paid and volunteer personnel; they include Greenpeace, Amnesty International, and the Red Cross. Finally, some have only one or two employees, with all other work being conducted by volunteers. They are, at bottom, grassroots associations that have grown complicated enough to justify paying someone to help with some of the group's routine operations that its volunteers are unable or unwilling to carry out.

Leisure service organizations are not voluntary groups, as just defined. Rather, they are collectivities consisting of a paid staff who provide one of more leisure services to a targeted clientele. To be sure, the clients are engaging in particular leisure activities, but the organizations providing them are not themselves leisure organizations of the sort considered in this section. Leisure service organizations are established either to make a profit, the goal of many a health spa, amusement park, and bowling center, for example, or in some instances, to simply make enough money to continue offering their services. This is the goal of charitable, nonprofits like Meals on Wheels, the YMCA and YWCA, and the Road Scholar (formerly Elder Hostel) Programs as well as governmental leisure and recreational programs and services.

DOI: 10.1057/9781137569943.0009

The next type of organization germane to leisure has already been considered; the social world was described in Chapters 1 and 5. Let me now add that the richest development of social worlds is usually observed in serious leisure, and if found at all in casual and project-based leisure, they are, by comparison, of much simpler composition. The casual leisure tribe may someday be shown to be the most complex formation among these two.

What remains, then, to be examined in this section on leisure and organization is the social movement. A social movement is a noninstitutionalized set of networks, small groups, and formal organizations that has coalesced around a significant value, which inspires members to promote or resist change with reference to it. The first question is whether participation in a social movement is a leisure activity. The answer is both yes and no, for it depends on the movement in question. Movements abound that gain members through their own volition, suggesting that the members experience no significant coercion to become involved. Some religious movements serve as examples, as do movements centered on values like physical fitness and healthy eating. Still, the latter two also include people who feel pressured by outside forces to participate, as when their physician prescribes exercise and weight loss or face an early death. Thus some social movements are composed of enthusiasts who are there for leisure reasons and other people who are compelled to be there (not leisure).

Finally, there are movements that seem to find their impetus primarily in people who feel driven to champion a particular cause, such as the celebrated temperance movement of early last century and the vigorous antismoking movement of modern times. A strong sense of obligation fuels participation in them. Those who make up the gun control and nuclear disarmament movements seem cut from the same cloth. Whether this is leisure must be determined empirically through direct research on the motivation of members.

Social movements, be they primarily of the leisure variety, the forced variety, or a combination of the two, have left a prominent mark on modern and postmodern life. Homer-Dixon (2007), for instance, commenting on the success of the mothers' movement in the 1960s that championed banning atmospheric nuclear testing, a practice that contaminated children's milk, now urges a similar formation fired by the goal of trying to bring global warming under control. Thus, considered alone, a social movement is a distinctive form of organization, which

DOI: 10.1057/9781137569943.0009

often provides serious and casual leisure for volunteers. Further, they are also likely to provide leisure projects for volunteers, enabling the latter to become involved for a limited period of time with a movement. Examples include participating in a fund-raising campaign, organizing a major rally, or lobbying for a crucial piece of legislation.

Caring and community involvement

Caring has been defined as the process of assuming personal responsibility for others' welfare, accomplished by acknowledging their needs and acting responsively toward them (Smith, Stebbins, & Dover, 2006, p. 34). According to Wuthnow (1991) caring is motivated, in substantial part, by compassion. Compassion leads to an inclination to show mercy for or give aid to – that is, to care for – one or more other people. Parrott (2001) delineates the emotional side of caring by classifying both it and compassion as tertiary emotions following from the primary emotion of love and the secondary emotion of affection.

Assuming a person is compassionate about another's situation in life and, as a result, wants to care for that individual, what roles and associated activities are open to the first? So far I have been able to identify three. One role is occupational; some workers who are compassionate about other people make a living, at least in significant part, by caring for them, something often done as a professional calling (e.g., clergy, physicians, social workers). Viewed from the angle of the SLP, many of these people would likely describe themselves as occupational devotees. Occupational caring is also community involvement, in the sense that all the collective serious pursuits contribute in this manner.

A second role, albeit one available outside work, is caring for other people as a personal obligation. Here the caring individual, fired by compassion, feels a moral duty to care for another person or class of people. Personal caring, as I will explain more fully in the next paragraph, is predominantly disagreeable; it is therefore not leisure. Rather it is the lot of those who, though they would rather be doing something else, find themselves caring, as an example, for an ailing relative or close friend or who feel morally pressed to aid the needy at home or abroad.

Here caring is a negative emotion aroused by a nonwork obligation.

DOI: 10.1057/9781137569943.0009

This brings up the question of whether communal expressions of such obligation are also instances of community involvement. My answer, which some readers may think debatable, is that these expressions are as, community involvement, marginal, primarily because the coerced nature of personal obligation signals an absence of voluntary altruism as defined in the preceding chapter. Otherwise, however, communal personal obligation seems to meet the six criteria for determining voluntary altruism.

Leisure caring is our third role. It refers to people engaged in uncoerced compassionate activity during free time, which they want to do and, in either a satisfying or a fulfilling way (or both), use their abilities and resources to succeed at doing (the general definition of leisure inherent in this statement was presented more fully in the Introduction). Both leisure caring and some kinds of personal obligation bear directly on community involvement. But leisure caring is differentiated from its occupational and personal counterparts by, among other qualities, the fact that it is undertaken only in free time.

Note that there may well be obligations in leisure caring, however, even while serious leisure research has demonstrated through several studies (reviewed in Stebbins, 1992) that the obligations felt there, because they are agreeable, are defined by committed participants as minor, as "minimal." But they are real nonetheless, even if the powerful rewards of the activity significantly outweigh them and the participant has the option to quit the activity at a convenient point in the near future. In other words, serious leisure has often been found to contain some flexible obligation, or a relative freedom to honor commitments. This condition is generally missing in occupational caring and personal obligation (a more extensive discussion of care as leisure is available in Stebbins, 2008).

There can be no doubt that leisure caring, using our definition, is a type of community involvement. Motivated by compassion and altruism, caring volunteers (they might be pursuing any of the three forms of leisure) arrange for some sort of beneficial contact with the target of their care. This might be a one-shot, perhaps, spontaneous act – a good deed – such as buying a homeless person a meal or giving first-aid to a pedestrian injured in a fall.[1] Or such care might be sustained over a period of time, as in ministering to a friend dying of cancer or helping out weekly at a local food bank.

Consistent with our definition of volunteering presented in Chapter 1, caring as volunteer activity is enacted beyond the volunteer's family. This condition means that leisure care within the family circle must be

DOI: 10.1057/9781137569943.0009

conceptualized in terms other than volunteering. Conceiving of it as special genre of family leisure – that is, as part of life there not experienced as disagreeable obligation – would be one way to achieve this.

Conclusions

It might be argued that contributing to the community as described here is something its members are obligated to do by dint of their citizenship in it. Margaret Somers defines citizenship as:

> a personal political status rooted in a set of universal rights that are enforceable by claims on the state and, historically, founded on the legal necessities of capitalist society and its government. Membership, participation, association, inclusion/exclusion, national identity, and the rule of law number among the core components of citizenship. (Somers, 1993, pp. 558 & 594)

Sometimes referred to as "active citizenship," this conceptualization includes not only rights but also responsibilities, commonly understood as feeling obliged to work toward improving community life.

This chapter shows that the "responsibilities" of active citizenship can be felt as a commitment to engage in a serious pursuit. Here, meeting these responsibilities is a leisure undertaking, even though such terminology might suggest that doing so is nonwork obligation.

Membership, participation, and association can be part of a lifestyle leading to fulfillment in a free-time activity. This is a community and organizational contribution made at the lofty heights of the commonweal.

Note

1 Good Samaritan acts of bystander intervention exemplify further this type of care (Darley & Latané, 1968).

References

Bott, E. (1957). *Family and social network*. London: Tavistock.

Darley, J.M., & Latané, B. (1968). Bystander intervention in emergencies: Diffusion of responsibility. *Journal of Personality and Social Psychology*, 8, 377–383.

DOI: 10.1057/9781137569943.0009

Helft, M. (2007). With tools on Web, amateurs reshape mapmaking. *New York Times*, July 27 (online edition).
Hemingway, J.L. (1999). Leisure, social capital, and democratic citizenship. *Journal of Leisure Research*, 31, 150–165.
Homer-Dixon, T. (2007). A swiftly melting planet. *The New York Times*, Thursday, October 4 (online edition).
Jeffries, V., Johnston, B.V., Nichols, L.T., Oliner, S.P., Tiryakian, E, & Weinstein, J. (2006). Altruism and social solidarity: Envisioning a field of specialization. *American Sociologist*, 37(3), 67–83.
Leadbeater, C., & Miller, P. (2004). *The pro-am revolution: How enthusiasts are changing our economy and society*. London: Demos.
Lyons, K., & Dionigi, R. (2007). Transcending emotional community: A qualitative examination of older adults and Masters' sports participation. *Leisure Sciences*, 29, 375–389.
Maffesoli, M. (1996). *The time of the tribes: The decline of individualism*, trans. by D. Smith. London: Sage.
Parrott, W.G. (Ed.) (2001). *Emotions in social psychology: Key readings*. New York: Psychology Press.
Pearce, J.L. (1993). *Volunteers: The organizational behavior of unpaid workers*, London, U.K.: Routledge.
Putnam, R.D. (2000). *Bowling alone: The collapse and revival of American community*. New York: Simon & Schuster.
Reid, D. (1995). Work and leisure in the 21st century: From production to citizenship. Toronto, ON: Wall and Emerson.
Rojek, C. (2002). Civil labour, leisure and post work society. *Loisir et Société/Society and Leisure*, 25, 21–36.
Smith, D.H. (2000). *Grassroots associations*. Thousand Oaks, CA: Sage.
Smith, D.H., Stebbins, R.A., & Dover, M. (2006). *A dictionary of nonprofit terms and concepts*. Bloomington, IN: Indiana University Press.
Somers, M.R. (1993). Citizenship and the place of the public sphere: Law, community and political culture in the transition to democracy. *American Sociological Review*, 58, 587–621.
Stebbins, R.A. (1992). *Amateurs, professionals, and serious leisure*. Montreal, QC and Kingston, ON: McGill-Queen's University Press.
Stebbins, R.A. (2002). *The organizational basis of leisure participation: A motivational exploration*. State College, PA: Venture.

DOI: 10.1057/9781137569943.0009

Stebbins, R.A. (2005). *Challenging mountain nature: Risk, motive, and lifestyle in three hobbyist sports*. Calgary, AB: Detselig (also available at www.seriousleisure.net/Digital Library).
Stebbins, R.A. (2008). The leisure basis of caring. *Leisure Studies Association Newsletter*, 79(March), 34–37 (also available at www.seriousleisure.net/Digital Library/ "Leisure Reflections no. 17).
Wuthnow, R. (1991). *Acts of compassion: Caring for others and helping ourselves*. Princeton, NJ: Princeton University Press.

DOI: 10.1057/9781137569943.0009

7
Quality of Life and Well-Being

Abstract: *The emotions of happiness, joy, hope, and optimism are covered, they being the most common accompaniments to high quality of life (QOL) and well-being. The subjective want-based approach to QOL is used as opposed to the objective social indicators approach. Of the three forms, serious leisure meets best the four components of QOL. These four can also be realized in many leisure projects, though the good QOL found there will be more evanescent, and possibly not even as sharply felt, as in the far more enduring pursuit of a serious leisure activity. Casual leisure can also help generate a decent QOL. To the extent that well-being is fostered by enjoyment of and satisfaction with the activities of everyday life, evidence suggests it is an important by-product of serious leisure. A discussion of happiness follows, and the chapter concludes with an examination of the aforementioned emotions.*

Keywords: casual leisure; happiness; hope; joy; optimism; project-based leisure; quality of life; serious leisure; well-being

Stebbins, Robert A. *Leisure and Positive Psychology: Linking Activities with Positiveness*. Basingstoke: Palgrave Macmillan, 2015. DOI: 10.1057/9781137569943.0010.

DOI: 10.1057/9781137569943.0010

We examine the following emotions in this chapter: happiness, joy, hope, and optimism. They are common accompaniments to the positive states of high quality of life (QOL) and well-being. In conceptualizing QOL, I use the subjective "want-based" approach to QOL, as opposed to the objective "social indicators" approach. The want-based approach consists of four components: "a sense of achievement in one's work, an appreciation of beauty in nature and the arts, a feeling of identification with one's community, [and] a sense of fulfillment of one's potential" (Campbell, Converse, & Rogers, 1976, p. 1). High QOL, however generated, is a state of mind, which to the extent people are concerned with their own well-being, must be pursued with notable attention. Well-being, in turn, emanates from a high QOL, as generated by some combination of the serious pursuits balanced with one or both of the other two SLP forms.

The plan for this chapter is first to examine QOL and then discuss well-being, both considered important constituents of positive psychology. Leisure, I will argue, significantly enhances each. The main emotions associated with these two states – happiness, joy, hope, and optimism – are considered next. Each emotion will be linked to the leisure activities that typically bring about its arousal.

Quality of life

Where does the SLP fit in the want-based approach to QOL? Of the three forms, serious leisure meets best its four components. The first – sense of achievement – is evident in serious leisure from what was said earlier about its rewards of personal enrichment, self-expression, group accomplishment, and contribution to the maintenance and development of the group as well as its qualities of career, effort, benefits, and perseverance that people can routinely find here. The second component, which refers to appreciation of beauty in nature and the arts, is found in such serious leisure forms as outdoor activities and artistic pursuits, including backpacking, cross-country skiing, sculpting, and playing string quartets.

Third, all serious leisure has links with the wider community, if in no other way, then through the social worlds of its participants. Additionally however, many serious leisure activities relate directly to the larger community, as through artistic performances by amateurs, interesting displays by hobbyists (of, e.g., stamps, model trains, show dogs), and needed services by volunteers. Sense of fulfillment of potential – the

DOI: 10.1057/9781137569943.0010

fourth component – comes primarily from experiencing the rewards of self-actualization, self-enhancement, and self-expression, but also, to a certain extent, from two distinctive qualities of serious leisure, namely, finding a career in the activity and having occasionally to persevere at following it. This close fit of serious leisure and QOL gives substance to John Neulinger's observation that:

> leisure is not just a component of the quality of life, but the very essence of it. It is not a neutral state of mind, but a positive, highly desirable one, and an important value. Leisure in my opinion is the guideline needed for any decision relating to the quality of life. (Neulinger, 1981, p. 66)

In other words, people find QOL, in part or in whole, through leisure experiences.

These four components can also be realized in many leisure projects, but the good QOL found there will be more evanescent, and possibly not even as sharply felt, as in the far more enduring pursuit of a serious leisure activity. Casual leisure, too, can help generate a decent QOL, although primarily through appreciating beauty in nature and the arts (e.g., subtype of sensory stimulation) and identifying with one's community (e.g., the subtype of casual volunteering). Finally, to arrive at an equally valid want-based conceptualization of QOL in devotee work, we need, in this statement, only to replace "serious leisure" with "devotee work."

High QOL, however generated, is a state of mind, which to the extent people are concerned with their own well-being, must be pursued with some care. (Did we not speak earlier of career, agency, and perseverance?) Moreover, high QOL does not commonly "fall into one's lap," as it were, but roots in desire, planning, and patience, as well as a capacity to seek deep satisfaction through experimentation with all three forms of leisure to eventually carve out an optimal leisure lifestyle (see Chapter 1). Human agency is the watchword here (discussed in Chapter 2). And we will see shortly that leisure educators, leisure/lifestyle counselors among them, can advise and inform about a multitude of leisure activities that hold strong potential for elevating QOL. Still, in the end, it is the individual who must be motivated to pursue them as well as develop and stick to a plan for doing this.

But, in this regard, not just any leisure activity or set of activities will do the job, as the idea of optimal leisure lifestyle demonstrates only too well. The highest QOL comes with developing an optimal leisure lifestyle, as understood in all the detail just presented. That is, the highest quality

DOI: 10.1057/9781137569943.0010

comes with a satisfying balance of serious, casual, and project-based leisure as defined by the person whose leisure life is being considered.

Quality of leisure life is influenced by, among other factors, the people with whom leisure participants pursue their leisure (Csikszentmihalyi, 1997, pp. 13–14) and even by the number and intensity – the quantity – of rewarding experiences found in this sphere of life (Neulinger, 1981, pp. 66–68). Csikszentmihalyi found that most people spend roughly equal amounts of time in three social contexts, and depending on how satisfying life is there, they also influence QOL. The first is composed of strangers, coworkers, coparticipants in leisure, and the like. The second is made up of one's family – parents, siblings, spouse (or partner), children, and so on. The third context is solitude, the absence of other people. It is quite possible that, since these three contexts are often settings for leisure activity, research will someday show that optimal leisure lifestyle, too, is influenced by how satisfying life is in them.

Well-being

The first question to pose in this section is whether an activity, even though freely chosen, can engender well-being when the first is encumbered with significant costs and a marginal status *vis-à-vis* the three domains of activity. The answer is that it can. For, to the extent that well-being is fostered by enjoyment of and satisfaction with the activities of everyday life, research evidence suggests that it is an important by-product of serious leisure (Haworth, 1986; Haworth and Hill, 1992; Mannell, 1993; Cuenca et al., 2014). Furthermore, when interviewed, the respondents in the studies of amateurs and hobbyists discussed in this chapter invariably described in detail and with great enthusiasm the fulfillment they get from their amateur and hobbyist activities. We might well expect to find the same reaction in the study of volunteers.

All this evidence is correlational, however. No one has yet carried out a study expressly designed to ascertain whether long-term involvement in a form of serious leisure leads to significant enduring increases in feelings of well-being. The extent to which serious leisure can generate major interpersonal role conflict for some practitioners – for example, it led to two divorces among the 25 respondents in the theatre study (Stebbins, 1979, pp. 81–83) – should be sufficient warning to avoid postulating an automatic link between this kind of leisure and well-being. I also have anecdotal evidence that serious leisure activities can generate intrapersonal conflict, such as when people fail to establish priorities among their many and varied leisure interests. Even an approach–approach conflict between two cherished leisure activities can possibly affect well-being unfavorably. Hamilton-Smith (1995, pp. 6–7) says our lack of knowledge about the link between serious leisure and well-being is a major lacuna in contemporary leisure research.

Finally, are we being realistic when we argue that serious leisure is a primary source of personal well-being in life? There is probably no sphere in life where well-being can take root and grow in pure, undiluted form. In other words, I suspect that when we are filled with feelings of well-being, whether at work, or during leisure, or while performing nonwork obligations, we are, in effect, experiencing those feelings as a significant profit of rewards against costs. Moreover, what is noteworthy about the theoretic link between any kind of leisure and well-being is that, in common sense, we seldom expect costs in the former, whereas we routinely expect them at work and during the execution of obligatory tasks. That we expect to find pure enjoyment everywhere in our leisure, however unrealistic, may be shown someday to have a powerful effect on how much we enjoy, are satisfied with, or happy about the serious leisure we pursue. And when a sense of well-being does emerge here – as it surely will – this expectation will influence the level of intensity with which the well-being is felt. Certainly, we can be mildly *or* highly satisfied with a serious pursuit or activity, enjoy it somewhat *or* enjoy it immensely.

Serious leisure and well-being would seem to make a perfect couple, but their relationship appears destined to be far more complex than current theory and research suggest. Part of that complexity roots in the relationship of well-being and citizenship. In this regard let us consider Keyes' (1998, p. 121) definition of *social well-being*: "an absence of negative conditions and feelings, the result of adjustment and adaptation to a hazardous world." For him well-being, though a personal state, is influenced by many of the social conditions considered earlier and incorporated in the SLP. Though the relationship is probably more complex than this, for purposes of the present discussion let us summarize in the following proposition what has been said to this point in this section: well-being emanates from a high QOL, as generated by some combination of serious leisure balanced with one or both of the other two forms.[1]

DOI: 10.1057/9781137569943.0010

As for citizenship our sense of being a citizen is itself an element in our social well-being, for this state is achieved, among other ways, through six components: membership, participation, association, inclusion/exclusion, national identity, and the rule of law (Somers, 1993, pp. 558 and 594). Moreover, the relationship of citizenship and well-being appears to be reciprocal, in that the latter helps make people good citizens. Diener and Tov (2007), in their study of social well-being, found that it varies widely across nations. They observed that, in general, it is associated with confidence in government and the armed forces, emphasis on postmaterialist values, support for democracy, lowered intolerance of immigrants and racial groups, among other factors. An elevated sense of social well-being, the authors concluded, correlates strongly with peaceful attitudes. Their results attest the strong reciprocity between well-being and citizenship.

Happiness

Interlaced among all the dreary news of the day are the persistent and mellifluous observations about happiness in our lives. Even though there is in this trendy interest a certain amount of phony and simplistic advice and thought, it is on the whole a good thing. At least it accents the positive and gets people thinking about their lives in such terms.

Richard Layard (2005, p. 12) defines happiness as the state of feeling good and enjoying life. It is a descriptive term. Moreover some thinkers see happiness as momentary: "[it] is considered to reflect a person's more temporary affective feelings of the present moment" (Mannell & Kleiber, 1997, p. 208). Examples include: "I was happy with my performance on the test," "I am happy that my party turned out so well," "I was very happy to receive that award the other day." Let us label this *short-term happiness*, so-called because the "present moment" might last a few minutes or even a few days.

By contrast, others see happiness as describing a broad swath of life, as expressed in such observations as: "I was happy as a child," "My years in this community have been happy ones," and "I will be happy in retirement." In this vein Diener (2000) holds that happiness and subjective well-being are the same. For him well-being is a combination of positive affect and general life satisfaction. Keyes' (1998, p. 121) definition of social well-being presented earlier harmonizes nicely with this proposition. To

DOI: 10.1057/9781137569943.0010

put the matter positively, let us say that well-being comes with having good health, reasonable prosperity, and, in general, being routinely happy and content. This is *long-term happiness.*

Short or long term, happiness is the result of a huge variety of personal and social conditions leading to this state in individuals (for a review of some of these, see Nawijn & Veenhoven, 2013, pp. 197–199). Thus, it is informative to describe people's (usually long-term) happiness, to know how many of them are happy, think they will be happy, once were happy, and so on. In this regard it is now common to compile national happiness ratings (see Datablog in *guardian.co.uk*, November 14, 2010), while Britain's Prime Minister, David Cameron, has decided to create a national happiness index. These are major undertakings, which by the way appear to ignore the short/long-term distinction just set out.

Yet even more complicated is the project of explaining such tendencies as well as explaining the condition of happiness itself. A substantial part of the explanation of happiness has been driven by the question of whether money makes people happy. In this respect economist Richard Layard (2005, p. 34) holds that, after about $20,000 (USD) in annual income, higher average income is no guarantee of greater happiness.

Subjective or social, the concept of well-being rests on the presupposition that, to achieve it, people must be proactive, must exercise personal agency to arrive at this state. Well-being is therefore also a goal, which when reached will demonstrate a person's overall happiness. The same may be said for obtaining a decent QOL. Both concepts speak to a process of personal betterment, as the individual defines this state. Happiness is therefore further explained by our willingness to work toward our own well-being and agreeable QOL. Moreover psychological and sociological positiveness (Stebbins, 2009) are sources of happiness. Happy people are positive about their lives, whether at the moment or over a long period of time.

The limits of the idea of happiness

Leisure can generate happiness, but is not itself happiness. Happiness is a state of mind; it is positive affect and a component of emotional well-being (Snyder, Lopez, & Pedrotti, 2011, pp. 128–139). By contrast leisure is activity; it is what we do in free time to make life attractive and worthwhile. We may describe ourselves as "happy," but we may not say we are "leisure" (however happy we may be).

DOI: 10.1057/9781137569943.0010

In general to be happy with a leisure activity is, at least in part, to be satisfied with it. Mannell and Kleiber (1997, p. 208) observe following Campbell (1980) that satisfaction implies a judgment, a comparison of the outcome of, for example, a leisure activity in the present with what the participant expected. Thus, low satisfaction with that activity would fail to generate happiness while in that state.

Casual leisure, because of its evanescent hedonism, is subject to losing its appeal and drifting toward low levels of satisfaction and short-term unhappiness, if not completely out of the zone into boredom. Frey's (2008) data from his study of television fit here. In addition, it is certainly possible that some kinds of sociable conversation lose their appeal after a protracted period of it. And most of us like to eat and sleep, but can become satiated with either after too much. In serious and project-based leisure participants may be dissatisfied, or unhappy, with how their activities or projects have turned out. The relatives get into a vicious quarrel at a family picnic; the soloist in the community orchestra concert, gripped with stage fright, plays badly off key; the board member of a nonprofit has at every meeting acrimonious exchanges with the organization's executive director. Some of these examples depict only short-term unhappiness, allowing thus for the possibility that long-term happiness in the activity remains high.

Happiness in leisure: Authentic or profound

Martin Seligman (2002) brings us to the jumping off point for relating leisure and long-term happiness, when he observes that "authentic happiness" comes from realizing our potential for enduring self-fulfillment. This observation opens the door to the central relationship that leisure has with happiness. Putting his thoughts into the SLP, we may say that enduring self-fulfillment springs primarily from serious leisure and devotee work activities, where it commonly takes several years to acquire the skills, knowledge, and experience necessary to realize this personal expression. Leisure projects are often capable of producing some sense of self-fulfillment, but not at the profound level of the serious pursuits. Casual leisure, because it is based, at the most, on minimal skill and knowledge, is incapable of producing self-fulfillment and therefore long-term happiness by means of it.

But there is reason to question Seligman's preference for the adjective "authentic." Is the happiness achieved through serious pursuits

DOI: 10.1057/9781137569943.0010

any more real or genuine than that achieved through casual leisure? Surely casual leisure happiness is real enough, as in the thrill of a roller coaster ride, an entertaining night at a comedy club, an enjoyable sociable conversation, or a bus tour offering breathtaking natural scenery. Rather, the central issue is how long does such happiness endure and how profoundly related is it to our personal history, acquired skills and knowledge, and special gifts and talents? Most leisure leads to real, authentic, happiness but only some of that happiness is profound, whereas some of it is comparatively superficial, falling thus at an intermediate point on the happiness–unhappiness dimension. Seligman, by the way, does not mention leisure in his discussion. Instead it is I who have extended his observation into free time and called into question the appropriateness of "authentic" as applied to happiness in the activities there.

Joy

Joy, says the *Shorter Oxford English Dictionary*, 5th ed. (2002), is "vivid pleasure arising from a sense of well-being or satisfaction." Robinson (2009) observes that it is an event-related emotion. Thus joy according to this definition is a kind of short-term happiness. Of the three forms of leisure it is most likely to be aroused during the casual form. But which types of casual leisure are prominent sources of joy?

Play often generates vivid pleasure, whereas relaxation seems unlikely to have this effect. Some entertainment is joyful, for example, comedy and winning at gambling. But would we qualify beating someone at cribbage, poker, or Chinese checkers as vividly pleasurable? Most, if not all, sociable conversation, though certainly agreeable, seems not to be especially joyful. Among the sensory stimulation varieties of casual leisure, those that are sexual and kinetic (e.g., carnival rides, river rafting) are probably the most likely to arouse joy. Hearing certain kinds of music can also be a joyful experience. As for casual volunteering and the pleasurable aerobic activities, they are rarely, if ever, experienced as joyful, as vividly pleasurable.

Experiencing joyful activities is an obvious and striking emotional component of QOL and well-being. The vast majority of these activities can be conceived of as casual leisure.

DOI: 10.1057/9781137569943.0010

Hope and optimism

Both of these emotions are central ingredients in high QOL and well-being. Moreover, both are oriented toward specific future outcomes, suggesting that both are long-term states. Hope, as defined here, is the expectation that the desired future outcome will occur. Optimism, on the other hand, is in this discussion the tendency to hope for the best. There is in optimism a sense of reasonable probability that the hoped-for outcome will result (e.g., I not only hope that I will be promoted but I am also optimistic that it will happen – c.f., Brown Kirschman et al., 2009, p. 137). There can be, however, hope without optimism (e.g., I hope I will be promoted, but I am not optimistic about this prospect). Thus there can be no optimism without hope, for there must be the expectation of the future outcome on which to base an optimistic assessment of it.

Hope and optimism are cardinal emotions in the serious pursuits and project-based leisure. Why, because these activities are engaged in using some combination of effort, skill, knowledge, and relevant experience. The goals sought here can only be reached when these personal acquisitions are effectively put into play. Thus, one might hope, even optimistically, to win a golf tournament, have a scientific paper accepted for publication, find a coveted rare coin for a collection, or be selected as a docent to teach at the local zoo.

Hope and, when warranted, optimism are in these complex leisure activities long term, because success in these fields (i.e., achieving desired outcomes) is channeled along lines of the leisure or leisure/work career (introduced in Chapter 1). In other words, hope is long-term in that the golfer hopes to improve to the point of generating better scores for each game and better performances in tournaments. The docent hopes to be selected to teach at the zoo and then to improve over time at delivering this kind of adult education.

Conclusion

Although leisure is not happiness it clearly plays a pivotal role in generating this state. We should never lose sight of this relationship with happiness, one of today's most vibrant spheres of life, for to do so would be to miss an opportunity to promote leisure's relevance to

DOI: 10.1057/9781137569943.0010

matters that count with science and the general public. Even if some (mostly casual) leisure leads only to short-term, relatively superficial happiness, it is nonetheless a kind of happiness many people seek. We in positive psychology should be showing them the many free-time avenues that may be taken to reach this goal and the nature of the benefits that may be found along the way. We should also plug serious and project-based leisure as additional routes to happiness, albeit of a more profound and enduring sort. In effect, we are arguing in doing this that, whereas money for most people is a poor currency for buying happiness (Layard, 2005, p. 34), leisure offers a much more profitable route to this goal. Serious and project-based leisure are far more likely to lead to long-term happiness, especially when, with the casual form, all three are integrated in an optimal leisure lifestyle.

Note

1 Brown Kirschman et al. (2009, p. 138) describe a similar relationship between QOL and "enhanced" well-being.

References

Brown Kirschman, K.J., Johnson, R.J., Bender, J.A., & Roberts, M.C. (2009). Positive psychology for children and adolescents: Development, prevention, and promotion. In S.J. Lopez & C.R. Snyder (Eds.), *The Oxford handbook of positive psychology* (pp. 133–148). New York: Oxford University Press.

Campbell, A. (1980). *The sense of well-being in America*. New York: McGraw-Hill.

Campbell, A., Converse, P., & Rogers, W.L. (1976). *The quality of American life: Perceptions, evaluations, and satisfactions*. New York: Russell Sage Foundation.

Csikszentmihalyi, M. (1997). *Finding flow: The psychology of engagement with everyday life*. New York: Basic Books.

Cuenca, J., Kleiber, D.A., Monteagudo, M.J., Linde, B.D., & Jaumot-Pascual, N. (2014). The influence of meaningful leisure on the subjective well-being of older adults in the Basque Country of Northern Spain. *World Leisure Journal*, 56(2), 120–129.

DOI: 10.1057/9781137569943.0010

Diener, E. (2000), Subjective well-being: The science of happiness and a proposal for a national index. *American Psychologist*, 55, 34–43.
Diener, E., & Tov, W. (2007). Subjective well-being and peace. *Journal of Social Issues*, 63, 421–440.
Frey, B.S. (2008). *Happiness: A revolution in economics.* Cambridge, MA: MIT Press.
Hamilton-Smith, E. (1995). The connexions of scholarship. *Newsletter* (Official newsletter of RC13 of the International Sociological Association), March, 4–9.
Haworth, J.T. (1986). Meaningful activity and psychological models of non-employment. *Leisure Studies*, 5, 281–297.
Haworth, J.T., & Hill, S. (1992). Work, leisure, and psychological well-being in a sample of young adults. *Journal of Community & Applied Social Psychology*, 2, 147–160.
Keyes, C.L.M. (1998). Social well-being. *Social Psychology Quarterly*, 61, 121–140.
Layard, R. (2005). *Happiness: Lessons from a new science.* New York: Penguin.
Mannell, R.C. (1993). High investment activity and life satisfaction among older adults: Committed, serious leisure, and flow activities. In J.R. Kelly (Ed.), *Activity and aging: Staying involved in later life* (pp. 125–145). Newbury Park, CA: Sage.
Mannell, R.C., & Kleiber, D.A. (1997). *A social psychology of leisure.* State College, PA: Venture.
Nawijn, J., & Veenhoven, R. (2013). Happiness through leisure. In T. Freire (Ed.), *Positive leisure science: From subjective experience to social contexts* (pp. 193–209). Dordrecht: Springer.
Neulinger, J. (1981). *To leisure: An introduction.* Boston, MA: Allyn and Bacon.
Robinson, D.L. (2009) Brain function, mental experience and personality. *The Netherlands Journal of Psychology*, 64, 152–167.
Seligman, M.E.P. (2002). *Authentic happiness: Using the new positive psychology to realize your potential for lasting fulfilment.* New York: Free Press.
Snyder, C.R., Lopez, S.J., & Pedrotti, J.T. (2011). *Positive psychology: The scientific and practical explorations of human strengths*, 2nd ed. Thousand Oaks, CA: Sage.
Somers, M.R. (1993). Citizenship and the place of the public sphere: Law, community and political culture in the transition to democracy. *American Sociological Review*, 58, 587–621.

DOI: 10.1057/9781137569943.0010

Stebbins, R.A. (1979). *Amateurs: On the margin between work and leisure.* Beverly Hills, CA: Sage (also available at www.seriousleisure.net – Digital Library).

Stebbins, R.A. (2009). *Personal decisions in the public square: Beyond problem solving into a positive sociology.* New Brunswick, NJ: Transaction.

DOI: 10.1057/9781137569943.0010

8

Casual and Project-Based Leisure

Abstract: *Casual leisure is fundamentally hedonic, pursued for its significant level of pure enjoyment, or pleasure. Its participants find, depending on the type of such leisure, an emotional world of joy, amusement, and attraction. By contrast, in the different kinds of leisure projects, positiveness roots in relatively short-term accomplishments and modest self-fulfillment (compared with the extensive fulfillment of the serious pursuits). Deferral of gratification is discussed, as is the pleasure principle. Entertainment, sociable conversation, and sensory stimulation are covered under the rubric of amusement. Attraction, a tertiary emotion, is considered with other tertiary emotions including adoration, fondness, liking, and caring. Joy is largely absent in project-based leisure, whereas amusement and attraction are commonly present there.*

Keywords: adoration; amusement; attraction; caring; casual leisure; hedonism; joy; liking; pleasure principle; project-based leisure

Stebbins, Robert A. *Leisure and Positive Psychology: Linking Activities with Positiveness.* Basingstoke: Palgrave Macmillan, 2015. DOI: 10.1057/9781137569943.0011.

When it comes to casual leisure, its participants find, depending on the type of such leisure, an emotional world of joy, amusement, and attraction. Casual leisure is fundamentally hedonic, pursued for its significant level of pure enjoyment, or pleasure. Indeed, this is the domain in life wherein people give expression in huge variety to Freud's pleasure principle. In the present chapter I explore this variety of positive leisure according to its eight types. I then turn to the different kinds of leisure projects, where positiveness roots in relatively short-term accomplishments and modest self-fulfillment (compared with the extensive fulfillment of the serious pursuits). The spatial contexts of both forms are also discussed and where relevant so is the body.

Casual leisure

In Freudian theory the pleasure principle was contrasted with its counterpart, namely, the human capacity to defer, or delay, gratification (see the pioneering "marshmallow experiment," Mischel, Shoda, & Rodriguez, 1989). Put in leisure terms, the serious pursuits offer a prominent arena for deferring gratification as participants make a long-term effort to acquire skill, knowledge, and experience sufficient to find, often many years later, deeply gratifying self-fulfillment. The leisure projects also require some deferral of gratification, but not to the extent done in the serious pursuits.

Deferral of gratification appears to be a process only rarely discussed in positive psychology.[1] Still, from what was said in the preceding paragraph with reference to this process and the state of fulfillment – which *is* a main concept in this branch of psychology – delaying gratification is vitally important. When harnessed with serious leisure and devotee work interests, deferring substantial rewards can hardly be ignored. And the study of the serious pursuits shows in concrete terms for each activity how deferral is accomplished.

All this, of course, has little to do with casual leisure and the pleasure principle, but rather it bears on the serious pursuits and our discussion of them in the preceding chapters as well as the leisure projects discussed later in this chapter. Nonetheless, the present chapter is the best place in this book to introduce the pleasure principle and to sharpen our understanding of it through comparison with deferred gratification as experienced in complex leisure.

DOI: 10.1057/9781137569943.0011

Joy

This emotion was introduced in the preceding chapter, cited there as an important component of quality of life and well-being. Vivid pleasure – the hallmark of joy – was said to be experienced primarily in casual leisure, particularly in the activities classified as play, entertainment, and sensory stimulation. But joy is evanescent, short term. As Eugene Field once noted: "All human joys are swift of wing, For heaven doth so allot it; That when you get an easy thing, You find you haven't got it" (http://www.quoteland.com/topic/Joy-Excitement-Quotes/706).

Amusement

Robinson (2009) notes that amusement is aroused by certain properties of an object. Parrott (2001) conceives of amusement as a tertiary emotion, an instance of the secondary emotion of cheerfulness. Cheerfulness, in turn, springs from the primary emotion of joy. Philosopher Roger Scruton (1982) elaborates on this basic conceptualization:

> Amusement is a mode of enjoying an object "for its own sake". My suggestion can be formulated in four propositions: (1) Amusement is a mode of reflective attention to an object. (2) It does not have the purpose of discovery (it does not concern itself with the acquisition of new beliefs, or the verification of old ones). (3) It is not a motive to action (it does not regard its object as the focus of any project or desire). (4) Enjoyment is to be explained by the thought of the object, and it is not felt (as Clark puts it) "for some ulterior reason". (p. 211)

Scruton's propositions jibe well with the observations that the emotion of amusement is often aroused by hedonic interests and is therefore consistent with the definition of casual leisure.

Not all of casual leisure is amusing, however, for casual volunteering and pleasurable aerobic activity are particularly unamenable to this emotion. By contrast play when defined as disinterested activity is obviously amusing. Though play will be examined in much greater detail in the next chapter, let us note here that Huizinga's (1955) famous definition of play squares nicely with Scruton's four propositions. Huizinga holds that play lacks necessity, obligation, and utility, being pursued with a disinterestedness that sets it, as an activity, apart from ordinary, real life.

DOI: 10.1057/9781137569943.0011

Examples include daydreaming, dabbling at an activity, and fiddling with something.

Is relaxation amusing? Probably not. Scruton's fourth proposition states that enjoyment (i.e., amusement) is to be explained by the thought of the object itself. To think about an "object" is to focus attention on it, to be engaged with it. In contrast, "relaxation is often a matter of bringing arousal down rather than up ... and often involves disengaging from more stimulating or stressful circumstances" (Kleiber, Walker, & Mannell, 2011, p. 113). Taking a nap, watching the flow of water in a river or creek, and observing the behavior of birds are usually relaxing, but not especially amusing.

Entertainment

On the other hand, both passive and active entertainment are expressly designed to amuse. Elsewhere (Stebbins, 2007) I have defined this genre of leisure as an object or occasion intentionally provided to a public for their enjoyment, or pleasure, that is meant to hold their attention for the period of time the object or occasion is perceived. Attention is directed, for example to a game, television program, rock concert, humorous picture, or fireworks display.

To understand more fully the idea of entertainment, we also need to identify and define its source. That source is the *entertainer*, defined here as a performer or other creator who, directly or indirectly (e.g., via film, TV, videotape), from a stage or equivalent, provides entertainment to a public. The equivalent may be an atelier, where for example, a sculptor, painter, or writer creates an entertaining (often humorous) work.

Amusements are objects or events that are intended to amuse. They are not, however, always entertaining, as entertainment has just been defined. For it will become evident in the section on sensory stimulation that amusements are also available on entertaining occasions.

Sociable conversation

Sociable conversations can be amusing, even while this feature is not an essential quality of these interchanges. When they are amusing it is often because they are humorous, generating gaiety among the participants.

DOI: 10.1057/9781137569943.0011

So bantering, telling jokes, recounting funny anecdotes, humorously describing a thing or event, and the like are the stuff of amusing sociable conversations.

Nevertheless, such conversations are not always amusing. A participant might without humor describe a serious event (e.g., car accident, night in the emergency room in a hospital, death of a pet). Discussions of the weather and sport – two time-worn subjects of many sociable gatherings – can be held in an atmosphere of gravity, perhaps even worry. Furthermore, gossip is sometimes deadly serious. Of course, to the extent that such concerns take over the conversation, it begins to lose its positiveness, even if it may still be characterized as sociable.

Sensory stimulation

The amusements providing sensory stimulation not definable as entertainment are legion. Theme parks are full of them: dizzying rides, fantastic displays, incredible acts, and so forth. Elsewhere, we are amused (or at least are supposed to be) while engaging in white water rafting; walking a via feratta; riding a funicular, gondola, or zip line; taking a bungee jump; and similar breath-taking experiences in a natural setting, albeit one typically modified in some way for our pleasure.[2]

Here the participant's body figures prominently in the amusement, doing so primarily through kinetic sensations experienced in space. Emotion is aroused through agreeable feelings of that person's body in controlled motion through space in unusual ways. Indeed, the space itself is most unusual, in that few people, without availing themselves of the amusement, can experience it from the angle that this space provides.

Attraction

As an emotion attraction consists of wanting to be near a person, animal, or object. Parrott (2001) considers it a tertiary emotion, with which he groups other such tertiary emotions as adoration, fondness, liking, and caring. The secondary emotion related to this set is affection, which is in turn an expression of the primary emotion of love (the latter also has other secondary and tertiary emotions). Attraction can be experienced in all eight types of casual leisure.

DOI: 10.1057/9781137569943.0011

In play people are attracted to – they experience attraction toward – the objects, animals, and people they want to play with. For instance, children wanting to play may be attracted to playground facilities, the family pet, their parents, or certain household objects (e.g., pots and pans, vase filled with flowers, a children's book). Adults in a playful mood might be attracted to a pencil and paper with which to doodle, a stick to throw for a dog who will fetch it, or an object with which to fiddle (e.g., hair, clothing, jewelry, Styrofoam coffee cups).

Attraction to objects can be aroused in conjunction with a desire to relax. Beds and easy chairs constitute two common examples. Some people are attracted to a beach where they relax while sun tanning or to a crackling fire for the relaxation provided by its warmth and mesmerizing flame. Boats and canoes lazily rowed or paddled are attractive for the relaxation this activity can offer the participant. The spaces in which these attractive objects exist are also appealing, as with the lake for paddling or sun tanning and the room with the bed or easy chair.

In entertainment, attraction is often felt toward the devices that provide it, assuming in this instance that they operate effectively. I have in mind here the likes of television sets, iPods, tablets, computers equipped with Internet service, CD players, and many more. Further, people can be attracted to the establishments that provide entertainment, including jazz clubs, concert halls, cinemas, casinos, race tracks, sports stadia, book stores, and libraries.

The main objects of attraction in sociable conversation are its participants. Other tertiary emotions in Parrott's (2001) list may also be aroused in these gatherings, depending on the subject being considered and the people involved. Thus, they may also feel adoration, affection, fondness, or caring for one or more of the others present. Lust and desire might even be aroused.

In the area of sensory stimulation, we can feel attraction for beautiful natural phenomena such as waterfalls, seascapes, mountains, birds and animals, and gardens. There is also the sensory stimulation gained through sexual activity and its myriad expressions. Where two (or more) people are involved in such activity, most of the senses are commonly aroused: sight, sound, smell, touch, and possibly even taste. Here, clearly, the object of emotional attraction is the other person and is augmented some or all of the time with the allied emotions of love, lust, desire, passion, and the like.

The principal attraction in casual volunteering is, in the case of the popular type, the target of benefits (e.g., the people served at the food bank, given directions at the museum, receiving snow-shoveling services from a volunteer). In faunal volunteering the animals (birds, reptiles, etc.) cared for are attractive, as are certain plants and trees in floral volunteering. Material volunteers can become attracted to the object of their benefits, among them, the historic house or battleground they are trying to preserve or the original character of an old neighborhood in their city they are striving to maintain. Casual environmental volunteers get attracted to the hiking trail they are helping to maintain or the municipal park they are trying to keep litter-free.

Pleasurable aerobic activity can also have its objects of attraction. Ordinary walking is such activity, to the extent that it elevates heart rate, though not beyond the point where the experience becomes too effortful. The routes taken during the walk may become attractive, in part through their association with this kind of leisure. The videotape that presents exergames could be an attractive object, because it provides a way to engage in agreeable activity (see http://exergamefitness.com, retrieved June 22, 2014).

Project-based leisure

Unlike immediately enjoying casual leisure, engagement in a leisure project does involve a measure of delayed gratification. Simply put, enthusiasts here must wait until the project is complete to enjoy to the fullest the fruits of their efforts. One noteworthy emotional outcome is the relative absence of joy in such endeavors.

Joy

This emotion, though rare in project-based leisure, seems most likely to be aroused in such activities as one-shot tours born of a fascination with a particular part or aspect of the world, be it Paris, polar bears, or the Peruvian Andes. Vivid pleasure can be experienced in, for instance, visiting Notre Dame in Paris or seeing at close range the bears frolicking with one another. Other examples include one-off balloon and cave tours and parachute jumps (some instruction required here).

DOI: 10.1057/9781137569943.0011

Amusement

This emotion, in contrast with that of joy, is a prominent feature of many leisure projects. Thus, in making something (e.g., a macramé plant holder, wooden decorative box assembled from a kit) the object made can arouse amusement in the maker. The same holds for successfully completed do-it-yourself projects such as finishing a room in the basement, building a boat, or planting a special garden. Repairs of, say, a malfunctioning dishwasher or faulty home wiring can also generate amusement in the finished project.

One-shot artistic projects are fecund sources of amusement for their creators. This is evident in home video, film, and slide shows as well as displays of photos. Mounting a skit, such as for an office party, family gathering, or birthday celebration, can be amusing for the producer(s) and it is hoped for the audience as well.

Attraction

Attraction is arguably the predominant emotion aroused by project-based leisure. All the making and tinkering projects revolve around objects that are by definition attractive to the hobbyist. It is likewise for the liberal arts projects, where for example, the developing genealogy or scrapbook becomes a captivating attraction for the family historian. Further, the objects of special tours are immensely attractive (e.g., the bears and church mentioned above) as are the books comprising such special projects as reading all Shakespeare's plays, all the Pulitzer Prize winners in letters and drama for a particular year or set of years, or all the novels having as their backdrop the industrial revolution.

One-shot volunteer projects often have their own attractions for the volunteers, exemplified mainly in events like conferences, arts festivals, and special exhibitions mounted in zoos, museums, and science centers. The aforementioned special home videos, films, slide shows, and displays of photos are attractive for those who create them. Finally, the memoirs that some people write have their own attraction. Found under this heading are the therapeutic audio, visual, and written productions of the elderly; life histories and autobiographies (all ages); and accounts of personal events (all ages). These projects are not to be confused with the diaries that many people keep, which amount to an ongoing form of relaxing casual leisure (Stebbins, 2014).

DOI: 10.1057/9781137569943.0011

Conclusions

The three emotions considered in this chapter, namely, joy, amusement, and attraction, can be aroused in casual and project-based leisure, albeit not uniformly so. From a therapeutic standpoint, particularly that of Rogerian, client-centered practice, it is good to know where in these two forms of leisure people may expect to experience which emotions.

Let us consider joy. Its vivid pleasure – the essence of this emotion – has been portrayed in this chapter and the preceding one as experienced primarily in casual leisure. Practitioners seeking joyful occasions for their clients will want to steer them toward activities that are playful or entertaining or that stimulate the senses. Nevertheless, joy in these activities is evanescent, hence a therapeutic strategy best used in combination with ones having more enduring positive effects.

Amusement, when used therapeutically, has as a short-term, casual leisure approach the same limitations as joy. Indeed, the former is found in entertainment and sensory stimulation just as the latter is. Amusement, however, can be aroused in sociable conversation, whereas this is improbable with joy. It was observed earlier that such gatherings are often amusing because they are humorous, they generate gaiety among the participants. So bantering, telling jokes, recounting funny anecdotes, humorously describing a thing or event, and so on number among the ingredients of amusing sociable conversations.

Nonetheless, sociable conversations invariably offer what the leisure activities leading to joy do much less effectively, namely, these conversations facilitate human interaction. In themselves these events, as in all casual leisure, are fleeting. Yet, they may lead to the formation of more enduring interpersonal relationships founded on one or more of the positive emotions of acceptance, love, sympathy, and admiration/respect (discussed in Chapter 3). Thus sociable conversations can sometimes serve as a therapeutic gateway to a longer-term, positive amelioration of certain personal problems.

Amusement, as was just noted, is also a prominent feature of many leisure projects. Thus, making and repairing things and completing do-it-yourself and artistic projects, though they are one-shot interests, can nevertheless contribute to a sense of subjective well-being. Being amused, having one's attention agreeably riveted on an object for its own sake, is in itself therapeutic.

Attraction – wanting to be near a person, animal, or object – is often a corollary of amusement: we are attracted to people and things that are

DOI: 10.1057/9781137569943.0011

amusing. Attraction in casual and project-based leisure is broader than amusement, however, for the former is aroused in all types of leisure. This breadth gives therapists a fair range of short-term activities with which to help their clients.

Notes

1 Seligman, during his examination of happiness and well-being in *Flourish*, does briefly mention the idea (p. 116).
2 A via feratta is a protected climbing or walking structure built for tourist pleasure over terrain or space otherwise inaccessible to the uninitiated.

References

Huizinga, J. (1955). *Homo Ludens: A study of the play element in culture.* Boston, MA: Beacon. The original was published in 1938 in Dutch, with its first English translation appearing in 1950.

Kleiber, D.A., Walker, G.J., & Mannell, R.C. (2011). *A social psychology of leisure*, 2nd ed. State College, PA: Venture.

Mischel, W., Shoda, Y., & Rodriguez, M.L. (1989). Delay of gratification in children. *Science*, 244(4907), 933–937.

Parrott, W.G. (Ed.) (2001). *Emotions in social psychology: Key readings.* New York: Psychology Press.

Robinson, D.L. (2009). Brain function, mental experience and personality. *The Netherlands Journal of Psychology*, 64, 152–167.

Scruton, R., & Jones, P. (1982). Laughter. *Proceedings of the Aristotelian Society, Supplementary Volumes*, 56,197–228.

Seligman, M.E.P. (2011). *Flourish: A visionary new understanding of happiness and well-being.* New York: Free Press.

Stebbins, R.A. (2007). The sociology of entertainment. In C.D. Bryant & D.L. Peck (Eds.), *21st century sociology: A reference handbook*, Vol. 2 (pp. 178–185). Thousand Oaks, CA: Sage.

Stebbins, R.A. (2014). Keeping a personal diary: Making time for relaxing contemplation. *Leisure Studies Association Newsletter*, 97(March), 30–32 (also available at www.seriousleisure.net/Digital Library, "Leisure Reflections No. 35").

DOI: 10.1057/9781137569943.0011

9
Play and Creativity

Abstract: *Play is a distinctive kind of positive behavior, whereas creativity is a distinctive positive process. Leisure studies and the study of play should be natural partners in the investigation of free-time activity. The scope of the two fields is examined and their central concepts defined. Much of theory and research in the social scientific study of play falls into three concentrations: (1) play as disinterested activity; (2) play as interested activity in games, both sport and nonsport; and (3) play as interested activity in the arts. Next, play is placed within the serious leisure perspective. Creativeness is treated as positive leisure activity, an offspring of the marriage of the studies of play and leisure.*

Keywords: art; casual leisure; creativity; dabbling; fun; play; science; serious leisure; sport

Stebbins, Robert A. *Leisure and Positive Psychology: Linking Activities with Positiveness*. Basingstoke: Palgrave Macmillan, 2015. DOI: 10.1057/9781137569943.0012.

Play (a distinctive variety of behavior) and creativity (a distinctive process) have found their place in positive psychology. The second, however, cuts a somewhat bigger figure there than the first. For Snyder, Lopez, and Pedrotti (2011, p. 66) note that "the benefits of competitive and noncompetitive adult play have not been delineated, and this topic is ripe for more research." That said, psychologists have extensively studied childhood play.[1] As for creativity Simonton (2009) devotes an entire chapter to the subject. He observed: "it is impossible to imagine the emergence of a bone fide positive psychology that does not include creativity among its topics" (Simonton, 2009, p. 262).

This chapter will take a different tack from the others in this book, in that neither the study of play nor the study of leisure has theoretically joined these two concepts. That is, it must first be shown how these two intellectual traditions blend with and complement one another before it can be argued that play is a kind of leisure capable of generating creativity. In other words, I intend to show how play and leisure together constitute a major source of creativity, a proposition of major importance for positive psychology. The main relevant emotions here are pride and fulfillment, possibly mixed with surprise (Oatley, Keltner, & Jenkins, 2006, p. 52). They will be discussed in the Conclusion.

Leisure and play

These two fields – leisure studies and the study of play, or play science – would be one might think natural partners in the investigation of free-time activity. For example, both set themselves off from the domain of work, albeit this distinction in both disciplines has sometimes been crudely conceptualized (I'll return later to this point). Both have had to battle the headwinds of naïve lay public imagery, which sees them as dealing exclusively in the frivolous. Yet, both have generated through research practical lessons of great import.

If we may thus conceive of leisure studies and the study of play as riding in the same scientific canoe, it is also true that they are mostly unaware of each other's presence there. The one in the bow (it makes no difference which one) paddles in directions unbeknownst to the one in the stern and vice versa. I suspect that it is because of this preoccupation with paddling their own disciplinary canoe as though no one else were aboard that this mutual ignorance has taken root and thrived. In

DOI: 10.1057/9781137569943.0012

general, members of the two fields know little about what their counterparts at the other end are doing. As evidence it is rare in the study of play to see words like "leisure" and "recreation" ("fun" is a common term, though), while in leisure studies "play," though appearing relatively more frequently, is hardly a household word.[2]

The scope of the two fields

The goal of any definition is to set out its essential features, thereby distinguishing the definiendum from everything else. Since such efforts are uncommon when it comes to defining play, Edward Norbeck's definition is especially welcome. His is a provisional statement, provisional in that future thought and research could prompt changes to it. He holds that play is "behavior resting upon a biologically inherited stimulus or proclivity, that is distinguished by a combination of traits: play is voluntary, somehow pleasurable, distinct temporally from other behavior, and distinct in having a make-believe or transcendental quality" (Norbeck, 2013, p. 1). He goes on to note that many definitions of play include the condition that it is nonutilitarian. Observing that this may not always apply to professionals in art and sport, he prefers to say that "at least among non-professional players, the goals of play are usually not consciously utilitarian" (p. 2). He states further that there is in play "a transcendence of ordinary cognitive states which ... seems to represent altered neurophysiology in a distinct and distinctive physiological state." Kimberlee Bonura (2009) adds that play is self-initiated, self-ended, and open-ended, thereby falling at the opposite end of a continuum starting with the domain of work. Furthermore, play activities have a beginning and an end. Nonetheless, I will argue later that these definitional statements need qualifying in certain respects.

That play is defined as a kind of behavior is not to imply that the latter is necessarily physical. True, we can physically play or dabble with an object or an organism, including those that some other people approach seriously (e.g., a piano, microscope, or food on a plate). Yet, it appears that most play is mental behavior, as seen most vividly in the creative, innovative manipulation, both conscious and semiconscious, of certain ideational elements leading thereby to new constructs of immense variety. These ideas may be expressed in, for instance, daydreams, stories, pretend play, and solutions to problems (including serious ones). Artistic

DOI: 10.1057/9781137569943.0012

and scientific creativity and strategies for winning games and sporting competitions also exemplify this kind of play. Consonant with this mental behavior thesis is one of the *OED*'s many definitions of play: "3 *fig.* & *gen.* Action, activity, operation, working, esp. with rapid movement or change, or variety. (Now almost always of abstract things, as fancy, thought, etc.)." Thus it should come as no surprise that the study of play revolves substantially around its psychological and neurological roots in humans as well as, recently, those found in other mammals in whom play behavior has also been observed.

And, speaking of the *OED*, it shows that the word "play" and its derivatives are awash in different meanings and usages. Play occupies nearly two full (dictionary-sized) pages in the *OED*. By contrast, "leisure" gets approximately four inches in one column and "recreation" about half of that (there are three columns per page). So, according to that dictionary, we might also play idly with an object, play a game of rugby, play on another's sensitivities, play the flute, and make a play for something, to mention a few meanings.

The scope of the study of play is determined substantially by the fact that one of its central concepts is a verb (play is also a noun). Moreover, it is several centuries old (the *OED* traces it to Old English). As a result plenty time has elapsed during which its users have piled on new meanings, subtle distinctions, pithy sayings, and lively metaphors. Moreover, because play is both a transitive and an intransitive verb, the range of its usage is still further extended and enriched.

This linguistic evolution has resulted in an amorphous, if not ambiguous, assemblage of ideas and, it seems, a veritable challenge to play scientists trying to convincingly adumbrate their field of inquiry and define its central concepts (e.g., Henricks, 2006, pp. 2–4).[3] Brian Sutton-Smith (2001) holds that the very idea of play is "ambiguous." Granted, some play scholars have little interest in a clear definition of the study of play as a field or even of its central concept, maintaining instead that open-endedness here is advantageous. They argue that it facilitates the exploration of frontiers and discovery of new ways of conceiving of play and its consequences.

By contrast leisure is a noun only. That is, we cannot "leisure," notwithstanding John Neulinger's (1981) attempt to introduce a new verb in his book *To Leisure*.[4] As a word leisure is at least as old as that of play, yet it cannot come anywhere near matching the proliferation of meanings of the latter. Compared with those who study play, leisure studies scholars,

DOI: 10.1057/9781137569943.0012

in attempting to determine the essence of their central concept, have had many fewer allied meanings, distinctions, sayings, and metaphors to contend with.

Therefore definitions of leisure abound (for a sample see Kelly, 1990, pp. 16–23). Moreover, they do not always agree. Indeed, I found the definition of leisure if done thoroughly required a small book (Stebbins, 2012). The short definition published there is reproduced in the Introduction of the present volume. Yet, definers of play face a much greater challenge in trying to nail down the essential definitional elements in their field's far more complex accumulation of usages.

Play: Concentrations of research and theory

Much of theory and research in the social scientific study of play falls into three concentrations: (1) play as disinterested activity; (2) play as interested activity in games, both sport and nonsport; and (3) play as interested activity in the arts.[5] The play of children within these three has attracted considerable scholarly attention, especially in psychology. Huizinga's (1955) famous definition of play falls primarily in concentration 1, though he also sees the arts (3) in these same terms. He says play lacks necessity, obligation, and utility, being pursued with a disinterestedness that sets it, as an activity, apart from ordinary, real life. Examples include daydreaming, dabbling at an activity, and fiddling with something.

Concentrations 2 and 3 fall at the end of a continuum identified by Roger Caillois (2001) as *ludus*, or rule-governed activity. The latter did not include 3 in his discussion, however, because art, as with work, creates wealth (Caillois, 2001, p. 5). On the other hand, he did regard hobbies as playful. At the other end of his continuum lies *paidia*, the play of concentration 1. In the study of play Huizinga's conceptualization has been rather more influential than that of Caillois. Concentration 1 might even be viewed as a pure type of play.

Concentrations 2 and 3 juxtaposed with concentration 1 reveal some logical difficulties, for the first two show that play activity is neither always disinterested nor wholly open-ended. Games have rules, which constrain what participants may (playfully) do in them. Likewise, in much of amateur and professional art, creativity is constrained by canon, by a set of aesthetic criteria embraced and promulgated by the

DOI: 10.1057/9781137569943.0012

art's establishment (in music, painting, theater, dance, craftwork, etc.). Play in games, sport, and art is also interested, goal-oriented activity. Furthermore, in these second two concentrations, though there may be no utility, there is, especially in team-based activity, obligation (e.g., obligation to members of the team). The fact that some activities in games, sport, and art are pursued as devotee work muddies further the conceptual waters of the study of play. Here, these workers play just as their amateur counterparts do, doing so, however, in service of their livelihood.

These concentrations of research and theory in the study of play are perfectly defensible, given how the verb play has been used in these three ways for centuries. And, to the extent that activities pursued in the three concentrations allow for the imaginative *play* of ideas, the study of play can surely contribute to our understanding of those activities. Even where play is partly structured, as in concentrations 2 and 3, spaces exist where the mind is free to roam, to play. Thus, the chess player ponders the consequences of alternative moves of his pieces on the board and the composer considers different harmonic options for ending a movement of a symphony she is writing. This, to repeat, is the play of ideas.

In the study of play children at play are sometimes described as having "fun," which amounts to a sort of research operationalization of the concept of play. But here, too, common sense usage begets confusion. For "fun" is also sometimes used to describe what people (children, adolescents, adults) experience when doing activities not ordinarily considered play (Stebbins, 2004). Telling a friend that I had fun the other day while skiing or playing Dungeons and Dragons refers to feelings about two leisure activities of far greater complexity than the fun a child experiences in playground activities.

Moreover, play is not always positive for the player, as leisure is not always thus for the participant (Stebbins, 2009). Sutton-Smith (2001) writes that play can be destabilizing, destructive, or disturbing. He observed imaginative expressions of this nature in children's stories. And are not adults also capable of letting their imaginations run wild with negative as well as positive thoughts? The principal difference separating the two is that leisure, even when marred by occasional negative experiences, is positive activity overall. It is activity that people want to do. On the other hand, play can sometimes be both disagreeable and unavoidable. Is this kind of play even leisure?

DOI: 10.1057/9781137569943.0012

Play as leisure/leisure as play

In the SLP play is classified as a type of casual leisure (Stebbins, 2007/2015). There it is conceived of as concentration 1 and is therefore in harmony with Huizinga's approach. Concentrations 2 and 3, however, are treated of rather differently in leisure studies. In the SLP these are discussed as amateur or hobbyist serious leisure and, recently, as devotee work. Play according to concentration 1, if considered at all in these two, is conceptualized as dabbling. That is, some amateurs and hobbyists acquire their initial interest in their serious leisure by disinterestedly playing at, for example, hitting a tennis ball, picking out notes on a piano, or drawing something (Stebbins, 2014).

Here leisure studies and the study of play overlap, even while apart from the word play itself, their theoretic terminology tends to be different. Thus it is possible to view play as a special activity pursued within the many leisure activities that foster it. More precisely, *Play activity* – it *is* an activity with a beginning and an end, both initiated by the participant – occurs as part of the core activity of a larger, or general, leisure activity (the core-general distinction is discussed in Stebbins, 2009).

By way of illustration, consider painting as a general leisure activity, the core activity of which is for certain painters portraying a still life of flowers. The play activities in the core (there will be several) are evident in the artist's expressing on canvas a personal interpretation of the flowers' color, arrangement, backdrop, and the like. Nevertheless, the general activity comprises more than its component play activities, for the artist must also select the best brush for the job, ensure that the ambient lighting is adequate, and assemble all the colors of paint needed for (playfully) mixing the final shades to be placed on the canvas. Play activities, specialized as they are, drive and motivate – they are enormously fulfilling – the spur-of-the-moment maneuvers in sport, interpretations in music, choices of words in creative writing, implications of exploratory data in science, artistic renderings of raw craft material, among many other possibilities in the serious pursuits.

But, just as critical, these spur-of-the-moment activities are not only playful but also creative, inventive, or novel – however one might describe this process of producing something new. In this regard Simonton (2009, p. 265) distinguishes between "small-c creativity [which] enhances everyday life and work with superior problem-solving skills" and "big-C creativity [which] makes lasting contributions to culture and history."

DOI: 10.1057/9781137569943.0012

The latter appear to fall primarily in concentration 3, whereas the former seem to be found mostly in 2. The SLP describes and explains the many different leisure activities that foster these two types of creativity.

It is when these play activities are conducted in concentrations 2 and 3 that we see most clearly how the studies of play and leisure complement each other and how creative processes are a main outcome. Here the psychology, neurophysiology, and ethology of play are central interests, interests that nevertheless have attracted rather few leisure studies scholars (but see Kleiber, Walker, & Mannell, 2011). Leisure studies specialists are primarily concerned with the more encompassing core and general activities, what motivates people to pursue them, the social–cultural–historical context of the activities, the consequences of the activities for participants and society, and so on. As one of a multitude of free-time activities, play in leisure studies has had no special status.

Nevertheless, leisure studies and positive psychology could benefit handsomely from recognizing the importance of play and incorporating it into theory and research. In the study of play, play is seen mainly as a process underlying those parts of the pursuit of a leisure activity where it can find expression, this being especially evident in concentrations 2 and 3. Sutton-Smith (2001, p. 4) provides a nine-fold classification of such activities, a list that has a number of counterparts in the classification of activities in the SLP (see figure 1.1, p. 13). Play – consciously or semiconsciously generating, identifying, and weighing ideas and choices – is in this, its essential sense, invariably imaginative, creative. Therefore play can contribute hugely to the rewarding pursuit of those leisure activities that encourage it, resulting in for instance, a wonderfully written passage of poetry, brilliantly executed set of athletic maneuvers in basketball, or exquisitely flavored sauce in cooking. Scientific interest in leisure's core activities should include these playful moments, and their inspiring, fulfilling ramifications. Herein lies the complementarity of the two fields.

Conclusions

Engaging in creative activity is often accompanied by an emotional response to it. Pride and fulfillment (both introduced in Chapter 2) are common when the creation or invention is laudable and possibly or actually open to evaluation by critical observers. Moreover, surprise

DOI: 10.1057/9781137569943.0012

may occur, a sort of "I-can't-believe-I-did-that" reaction to the creative movement, product, idea, and the like. The emotion of surprise in these instances is positive, though as Snyder (2002) points out, we can also be surprised at negative events.

Creativeness has been treated in this chapter as positive, an offspring of the marriage of play and leisure. Nonetheless, as noted earlier, Sutton-Smith (2001) finds that play can also be destabilizing, destructive, or disturbing in its creativeness, arousing negative emotions in its wake. Positive psychology's interest in creativity, and with this chapter the play/leisure source of the second, does not therefore fully explain either the origin of creativity or its emotional accompaniments.

Notes

1 See Questia's extensive list of publications on the psychology of play, all them centered on children: http://www.questia.com/library/psychology/other-types-of-psychology/psychology-of-play (retrieved July 4, 2014).

2 Most leisure studies textbooks say little or nothing about play. The encyclopedias and handbooks follow a similar pattern (but see Moore, 2003). The richest discussion of play within the field of leisure studies is found in its social psychology, most notably that of Kleiber, Walker, & Mannell (2011). And, as noted in fn1, the psychology of childhood play is well developed.

3 Norbeck (2013) observes that "scholars interested in [defining play] have been troubled in answering the question 'What is play?'"

4 Leisure studies has not embraced Neulinger's suggestion, however helpful it might have been (Stebbins, 2013).

5 The study of play is highly interdisciplinary and includes volumes on play and the brain and play in nonhuman animals.

References

Bonura, K. (2009). Academic learning and play. In R.P. Carlisle (Ed.), *Encyclopedia of play in today's society* (pp. 1–5). Thousand Oaks, CA: Sage.

Caillois, R. (2001). *Man, play and games*, trans. M. Barash. Urbana, IL: University of Illinois Press. The original was published in 1958 in French and translated into English in 1961.

DOI: 10.1057/9781137569943.0012

Henricks, T.S. (2006). *Play reconsidered: Sociological perspectives on human expression.* Urbana, IL: University of Illinois Press.
Huizinga, J. (1955). *Homo ludens: A study of the play element in culture.* Boston, MA: Beacon. The original was published in 1938 in Dutch, with its first English translation appearing in 1950.
Kelly, J.R. (1990). *Leisure*, 2nd ed. Englewood Cliffs, NJ: Prentice Hall.
Kleiber, D.A., Walker, G.J., & Mannell, R.C. (2011). *The social psychology of leisure*, 2nd ed. State College, PA: Venture.
Moore, K. (2003). Play. In J.J. Jenkins & J.J. Pigram (Eds.), *Encyclopedia of leisure and outdoor recreation* (pp. 373–376). London: Routledge.
Neulinger, J. (1981). *To leisure: An introduction.* Boston, MA: Allyn and Bacon.
Norbeck, E. (2013). The anthropological study of human play. http://www.dspace.rice.edu/bitstream/handle/1911/63156/article_RIP603_part1.pdf?sequence=1 (retrieved January 22, 2013).
Oatley, K., Keltner, D., & Jenkins, J.M. (2006). *Understanding emotions*, 2nd ed. Oxford: Blackwell.
Simonton, D.K. (2009). Creativity. In S.J. Lopez & C.R. Snyder (Eds). *The Oxford handbook of positive psychology*, 2nd ed. (pp. 261–269). New York: Oxford University Press.
Snyder, C.R. (2002). Hope theory: Rainbows in the mind. *Psychological Inquiry*, 13, 249–275.
Snyder, C.R., Lopez, S.J., & Pedrotti, J.T. (2011). *Positive psychology: The scientific and practical explorations of human strengths*, 2nd ed. Thousand Oaks, CA: Sage.
Stebbins, R.A. (2004). Fun, enjoyable, satisfying, fulfilling: Describing positive leisure experience. *Leisure Studies Association Newsletter*, 69(November), 8–11 (also available at www.seriousleisure.net/Digital Library, "Leisure Reflections No. 7").
Stebbins, R.A. (2007/2015). *Serious leisure: A perspective for our time.* New Brunswick, NJ: Transaction (paperback edition with new Preface, 2015).
Stebbins, R.A. (2009). *Personal decisions in the public square: Beyond problem solving into a positive sociology.* New Brunswick, NJ: Transaction.
Stebbins, R.A. (2012). *The idea of leisure: First principles.* New Brunswick, NJ: Transaction.

DOI: 10.1057/9781137569943.0012

Stebbins, R.A. (2013). *Homo otiosus*: Who is this creature, does it exist, should it matter? *Leisure Studies Association Newsletter*, 94(March), 19–21 at (also available at www.seriousleisure.net/Digital Library, "Leisure Reflections No. 32").
Stebbins, R.A. (2014). *Careers in serious leisure: From dabbler to devotee in search of fulfillment*. Houndmills, UK: Palgrave Macmillan.
Sutton-Smith, B. (2001). *The ambiguity of play*. Cambridge, MA: Harvard University Press.

DOI: 10.1057/9781137569943.0012

Conclusion

Abstract: *Can positive psychology develop a leisure wing? This is possible. Incorporating leisure in its analytic framework can only strengthen its role as the standard bearer for the vibrant, new positive approach in psychology. Nonetheless, not all of positive psychology can be related to leisure or exclusively to leisure. Several examples of positive emotions and interactive situations outside the realm of leisure are presented. As for the application of leisure in positive psychology, note that people can find positive meaning and purpose at work. As another example note that the serious leisure perspective sets out the different types of contemplation and spirituality, indicating where they are motivated by serious, casual, and project-based interests.*

Keywords: applied positive psychology; casual leisure; emotions; leisure; positive psychology; project-based leisure; serious leisure

Stebbins, Robert A. *Leisure and Positive Psychology: Linking Activities with Positiveness*. Basingstoke: Palgrave Macmillan, 2015. DOI: 10.1057/9781137569943.0013.

DOI: 10.1057/9781137569943.0013

By way of a wrap-up three points remain to be considered. They revolve around whether positive psychology can develop a leisure wing, the limits to the usefulness of the idea of leisure in positive psychology, and the role of leisure in applied positive psychology.

Leisure in positive psychology

Can positive psychology develop a leisure wing? Working against this possibility is the fact that leisure has not been, historically, a concept in mainstream psychology. Psychology's dictionaries contain no direct reference to leisure, even though psychologists do occasionally conduct research on leisure (positive psychology contains some exceptions to this general neglect, e.g., Freire, 2013). To be precise, what is known about leisure from the standpoint of psychology has been described as a "social psychology of leisure" and "a child of leisure studies" (Mannell, Kleiber, & Staempfli, 2006, p. 119). These authors hold that "leisure has all but been ignored by social psychologists in the field of psychology during the past 100 years" (pp. 112–113). So, by and large, the contributions to the psychological understanding of leisure motivation, experience, attitude, emotion, and personality have come from scholars appointed in leisure studies departments or allied units, among them, Seppo Iso-Ahola, Roger C. Mannell, and Douglas A. Kleiber.

It seems that psychologists outside leisure studies do not see leisure as a mental phenomenon, but rather as a sphere of life where such phenomena display certain distinctive features. In contrast the psychologists in leisure studies, being social psychologically oriented, do also see leisure as an abstract sphere – as an institution (see also Pt. 9 on "positive institutions," Lopez & Snyder, 2009). They are at ease with ideas like uncoerced behavior, core activity, free time, and types of leisure activity.

Leisure studies theory and research has influenced work in the social psychology of leisure. For example, Kleiber (2000) describes the role of casual leisure in facilitating relaxation. John Haworth (1997) notes that serious leisure helps generate psychological well-being. Mannell (1993) has studied the contribution of commitment and serious leisure to life satisfaction in leisure among older adults. Still, from the standpoint of institutional location, only Haworth, who until his recent retirement worked in a department of psychology, has managed to bridge both fields. The other two are appointed in leisure studies units.

DOI: 10.1057/9781137569943.0013

Nonetheless, leisure is an idea that is consonant with psychological research, as has already been shown in some of the psychological research carried out in leisure studies. Activity, defined as a set of behaviors, is a crucial conceptual linchpin in this process. The concepts of hedonic primary enhancements and eudaemonic primary enhancements (see Chapter 2) constitute two other linchpins.

In short, can positive psychology break the mold of its mainstream progenitor? I suspect it can, for it did just that in establishing the positive wing of the discipline in the first place. Incorporating leisure in its analytic framework can only strengthen its role as the standard bearer for the new positive orientation within psychology.

The limits of leisure in positive psychology

That said, not all of positive psychology can be related to leisure or exclusively to leisure. Thus, I have argued that optimism accompanies the serious pursuits, but have said nothing about an optimistic outlook associated with, for example, judicial proceedings, medical recovery, or a tax refund. It is likewise with wisdom, which can guide some serious pursuits but also many nonleisure interests, among them, settling family quarrels, dealing with a difficult superior, and buying a car or a house. And might we not say the same for courage, which is called for in, say, certain levels of whitewater kayaking or mountaineering as well as in confronting a colleague about that person's moral behavior or facing down a belligerent drunk.

Turning to the emotions often associated with volunteering – empathy, gratitude, and forgiveness, for example – they, too, can be found outside the leisure domain. Thus, we might empathize with a friend in pain from an accident, a person who has just been laid off because of a budget reduction, or someone whose house has just burned to the ground. As for gratitude it is often the emotion of the targets of volunteering, who in fact are not commonly seeking leisure when they receive such a service. Still, gratitude may also be expressed in response to actions of others taken outside the realm of leisure, as in being grateful for receiving a bonus at work or getting a ride while hitchhiking. Forgiveness was not covered earlier, because it is not a main emotion in leisure activities. And it may be shown that it is no more prominent outside that domain,

DOI: 10.1057/9781137569943.0013

exemplified in forgiving someone's tirade, insult, or grumpy mood at work.

Leisure and the application of positive psychology

I have said little about the application of positive psychology and the role leisure might play in this endeavor. To have done so would have expanded this book well beyond the size of the typical monograph, for such application constitutes an immense field (e.g., Linley, Harrington, & Garcea, 2013; Lopez & Snyder, 2009, Pt. 10). Let it suffice to observe that incorporating pertinent aspects of the SLP in the applications in positive psychology can often enhance considerably their effectiveness.

Let us look at two examples. Linley, Harrington, and Garcea (2013) focus in their collection on the ways that people can find meaning and purpose at work. From the angle of the SLP the most obvious link to the study of occupational meaning and purpose is through the concept of devotee work anchored as it is in serious leisure. Here the emphasis is on seeking self-fulfillment through core activities realized through perseverance, effort, and the acquisition of skills, knowledge, and experience. Here motivation springs in part from participating in an exciting social world, as carried out from a positive personal and social identity in a given activity.

Our other example is found in the realm of meditation and spirituality (see Shapiro and Pargament/Mahoney in Lopez & Snyder, 2009, chaps. 57 and 58). The SLP sets out the different types of contemplation and spirituality, indicating where they are motivated by serious, casual, and project-based interests. It also encourages consideration of the spatial aspects contemplation and spirituality as well as where these two are used to solve problems (i.e., the positive vs. the negative). Furthermore, the search for spirituality may become a leisure-based way of life.

Conclusion

Until positive psychology came along, leisure studies could justifiably claim to be the only positive social science. Martin Seligman, one of the founders of the former, stated that this new field was meant to develop into a "positive social science" (http://www.psych.upenn.edu/seligman/

DOI: 10.1057/9781137569943.0013

ppgrant.htm). This was to counteract the fact that many other social science disciplines tend to emphasize the negative rather than the positive side of human life.

But leisure studies can plead not guilty of this oversight, as charged for all the social sciences, since leisure studies is the only, essentially, *happy science* (Stebbins, 2007). This is true, notwithstanding a little list of negative emotions that occasionally creep into some leisure. People in the West, at least, are interested in the positive side of life, even while most of the social sciences are not. And to the extent that this interest is growing, the happy science and the positive wing of psychology will be well positioned, both theoretical and practically, to shed light and offer services on matters about which these people care a great deal.

References

Freire, T. (Ed.) (2013). *Positive leisure science: From subjective experience to social contexts.* Dordrecht, the Netherlands: Springer.

Haworth, J.T. (Ed.) (1997). *Work, Leisure and Well-Being.* London: Routledge.

Kleiber, D.A. (2000). The neglect of relaxation. *Journal of Leisure Research*, 32, 82–86.

Linley, P.A., Harrington, S., & Garcea, N. (Eds.) (2013). *The Oxford handbook of positive psychology and work.* New York: Oxford University Press.

Lopez, S.J., & Snyder, C.R. (Eds.) (2009). *The Oxford handbook of positive psychology*, 2nd ed. New York: Oxford University Press.

Mannell, R.C. (1993). High investment activity and life satisfaction among older adults: Committed, serious leisure, and flow activities. In J.R. Kelly (Ed.), *Activity and aging: Staying involved in later life* (pp.125–145). Newbury Park, CA: Sage.

Mannell, R.C., Kleiber, D.A., & Staempfli, M. (2006). Psychology and social psychology and the study of leisure. In C. Rojek, S.M. Shaw, & A.J. Veal (Eds.), *A handbook of leisure studies* (pp. 109–124). New York: Palgrave Macmillan.

Stebbins, R.A. (2007). Leisure studies: The happy science. *Leisure Studies Association Newsletter*, 76(March), 20–22 (also available at www.seriousleisure.net/Digital Library, "Leisure Reflections No.14").

DOI: 10.1057/9781137569943.0013

Index

DOI: 10.1057/9781137569943.0014

DOI: 10.1057/9781137569943.0014

DOI: 10.1057/9781137569943.0014

DOI: 10.1057/9781137569943.0014

DOI: 10.1057/9781137569943.0014

DOI: 10.1057/9781137569943.0014

DOI: 10.1057/9781137569943.0014

9781137569936